Historical Analysis Series

A PATTERN FOR JOINT OPERATIONS:
WORLD WAR II CLOSE AIR SUPPORT, NORTH AFRICA

by

Daniel R. Mortensen

*Office of Air Force History and
U.S. Army Center of Military History
Washington, D.C.*

Library of Congress Cataloging-in-Publication Data

Mortensen, Daniel R.
    A pattern for joint operations.

    (Historical analysis series)
    1. World War, 1939-1945--Campaigns--Africa, North.
2. World War, 1939-1945--Aerial operations, American.
3. Unified operations (Military science) I. Title.
II. Series.
D766.82.M63 1987   940.54'23   87-19335

CMH Pub 93-7

First Printing 1987

For sale by the Superintendent of Documents, U.S. Government Printing Office
Washington, DC 20402

FOREWORD

This study in the Historical Analysis Series examines a subject of importance not only to the Army but also to the Air Force: the origin and development of American close air support doctrine and practice in World War II. The idea for the study resulted from a review of the Memorandum of Understanding between the Army and Air Force chiefs of staff, concluded on 22 May 1984, and of the initiatives that emerged from that historic document, particularly Initiative 24, which reaffirmed the Air Force's mission to provide close air support to the Army. The project has been a cooperative effort between the U.S. Army Center of Military History and the U.S.A.F. Office of Air Force History; an Air Force historian was assigned to write the study under the supervision of the Center of Military History. The resulting work, ultimately the best judgment of the author based on historical evidence, is titled <u>A Pattern for Joint Operations: World War II Close Air Support, North Africa</u>. The concentration is on the North African campaign because that was the first major large-unit test of American ground armies in World War II, and in that campaign the basic system of close air support for American ground and air forces in World War II was first worked out.

Close air support doctrine both then and now is critical to the services. As this study demonstrates, the doctrine that had been conceived and practiced prior to the first American battles of World War II fell apart in the mud and fog of Tunisia. Both air and ground commanders in 1941 recognized the necessity of close cooperation between the staffs and forces in joint and combined forces. What they had to learn in 1942 was the degree to which close air support doctrine tested that cooperation and required alteration. The struggle of ground and air leaders to define and construct a command and control system, and ultimately to allocate and commit precious air resources to requisite ground missions, has as many lessons today as it did more than forty years ago.

We believe this study merits careful reading by all those who must plan and prepare for combat.

RICHARD H. KOHN
Chief
Office of Air Force History

WILLIAM A. STOFFT
Brigadier General, U.S. Army
Chief of Military History

Washington, D.C.
1 August 1987

THE AUTHOR

Daniel R. Mortensen, a historian with the Office of Air Force History, received his B.A. and M.A. in history from the University of California, Riverside, and a doctorate in 1976 from the University of Southern California (USC). He taught at several institutions in southern California, including USC, Pepperdine, and Loyola, and subsequently a course in aviation technology at the University of Maryland, College Park. Before coming to Washington in 1981, he served as deputy command historian of the Air Force Communications Command at Scott Air Force Base, Illinois. He specializes in the history of communications, aviation technology, and tactical aviation, and he has given papers on all these topics. In 1986 he was temporarily assigned to the U.S. Army Center of Military History, to write this study. Currently, he is completing a history of World War II tactical aviation for the Office of Air Force History.

PREFACE

In 1984 increasing concern about joint service operations occasioned the Chiefs of Staff of the United States Air Force and Army to investigate interservice cooperation. On 22 May Generals Charles A. Gabriel and John A. Wickham, Jr., signed an agreement to improve the battlefield cooperation between the Air Force and Army. The agreement recommended thirty-one topics, or areas, called the "31 Initiatives," for further investigation. In turn, Army and Air Force historians agreed that a study of the origins of modern close air support practices could help shed light on one particular initiative, namely, current close air support practices. After a preliminary investigation of research resources, the concept for this manuscript was redefined as a study of doctrinal formation and close air support practices during the important early phases of World War II. Archival records indicated that ground and air leaders had an abiding concern about the nature and practice of close air support in modern combined battle operations, and they compiled a long and rich record. This study combines research materials, including some newly discovered documents from both Army and Air Force archives, and it reflects as well the combined knowledge and effort of both Army and Air Force historians.

The story of events in Washington and North Africa between 1939 and mid-1943, when the Allies defeated Axis forces in Tunisia, has current significance. The interplay of staff planning and attempts to define doctrine, the organization of training and field operations, and adjustments to the demands of technology should be instructive. Generals George C. Marshall, Dwight D. Eisenhower, Henry H. Arnold, George S. Patton, Jr., Omar N. Bradley, Carl Spaatz, and other air and ground leaders were vitally concerned with the cohesiveness of their combined forces--that is, the shared understanding among the leaders in Washington and the commanders at theater and task force levels. Another aspect that may be of interest to Army students of close air support is the testing of War Department doctrine in the muddy terrain of Tunisia, under the constraints of "the fog of battle," that typified the Allied experience in North Africa. Air Force leaders may also find, at the very least, some value in the struggle to define command and control systems or in the attitudes of ground personnel, especially the latter's need to understand the commitment of air-to-ground tasks.

It is altogether fitting that this study of joint air-ground operations in World War II should recognize the early support of those Army and Air Force people who found a historical analysis to be important. Army Col. David Cooper and Air Force Lt. Col. Edward Land of the Joint Assessment and Initiative Office; Col. Ken Kissell of the Chief of Staff, USAF, Staff Group; Lt. Col. Robert Frank and Dr. Alexander S. Cochran, Jr., of the U.S. Army Center of Military History; and Mr. Herman Wolk and Col. Fred Shiner of the Office of Air Force History--each in their own way offered encouragement for the particular subject of close air support and to the idea of a cross-service research project.

Librarians and archivist at the U.S. Army Center of Military History and at the Office of Air Force History were particularly helpful. At the Center of Military History Miss Hannah Zeidlik, Ms. Barbara Williams, and Ms. Geraldine K. Judkins dug out historical documents and records and found books relating to the subject. Mr. William C. Heimdahl and M. Sgt. Roger A. Jernigan at the Office of Air Force History offered advice and unending effort to the search for materials. Finally, Mr. Hugh Howard, Mrs. Patricia Tugwell, and Mrs. Velma Jones at the Pentagon Library and archivists Mr. Edward J. Reese, Mr. Wilbert B. Mahoney, and Ms. Teresa Hammet at the Modern Military Branch of the National Archives and Records Administration provided valuable research assistance in my search for pertinent World War II records. Special thanks is due to these competent librarians and archivists for their continued professional service to demanding historians as myself.

All those who read and reread drafts of the manuscript deserve more recognition than given in these few lines of credit. Much thanks will remain in my heart. Nevertheless, my appreciation extends to many colleagues at the Center of Military History: Dr. David F. Trask; Lt. Col. Robert Frank; Dr. Alexander S. Cochran, Jr. ; Maj. Bruce Pirnie; Dr. Edgar F. Raines, Jr.; Lt. Col. David Campbell; Maj. Lawrence M. Greenberg; Maj. Francis T. Julia, Jr.; and Dr. Paul J. Scheips, who kept me honest with the Army viewpoint and corrected by grammar. At the Office of Air Force History important readers and advisers included Col. Fred Shiner, Mr. Herman Wolk, Dr. B. Franklin Cooling, Dr. George Watson, and Dr. Wayne Thompson. They all expended great energy and time in their critiques of the manuscript. Additional advice was continually sought from Dr. Fred Beck, Dr. Walton Moody, Lt. Col. Vance Mitchell, and Maj. John Kreis, whose knowledgeable minds helped expand my understanding of the very complicated events of World War II Washington and North Africa.

The individuals involved in the preparation of this study for publication also deserve special mention. At the Air Force they include: Dr. Fred Beck, Mrs. Anne E. Andarcia, Ms. Vanessa Allen, Mr. David Chenoweth, Ms. Laura L. Hutchinson, and Mr. Ray Del Villar. At the Army they include: Mr. John W. Elsberg; Mr. Arthur S. Hardyman; Ms. Linda M. Cajka who prepared the charts, maps, illustrations, and the cover; Mr. Robert J. Anzelmo, my editor; and last but really first, my project editor, Ms. Joanne M. Brignolo.

As expected, this writer takes full responsibility for interpretations, omissions, and errors of fact.

Washington, D.C. DANIEL R. MORTENSEN
1 August 1987

CONTENTS

	Page
PROLOGUE	3

Chapter

I. ORGANIZATION, DOCTRINE, AND WEAPONS FOR CLOSE AIR SUPPORT	6
The Interwar Years	6
Increasing Influence of the Air Arm, 1938-1942	9
Requirements for Hemisphere Defense	11
Requirements for War With the Axis	13
Doctrine for War	20
Aircraft: Enabling the Execution of Close Air Support	24
II. NORTH AFRICAN CLOSE AIR SUPPORT OPERATIONS	47
World War II Operations and North Africa	47
Planning Close Air Support for North Africa	50
Operations: TORCH Landings and the Offensive Against Tunisia	56
Operations: Reorganization and the Second Tunisian Offensive	62
Operations: Kasserine and a New Look at Close Air Support	70
Close Air Support After Kasserine	83
EPILOGUE	94

MAPS

No.		Page
1.	North Africa and the Mediterranean, 1942-1943	48
2.	TORCH Landings in Northwest Africa, 8 November 1942	54
3.	First Action in Tunisia, 16-23 November 1942	58
4.	Comparative Distances of Allied and Axis Airfields, December 1942	60
5.	American Battlefield in Southern Tunisia	64

CHARTS

1.	Channels of Tactical Control of Combat Aviation in Typified Air Support Command	21
2.	Allied Command Relationships in North Africa and the Mediterranean, March 1943	74

ILLUSTRATIONS

1.	Curtiss A-18s	29
2.	Douglas A-20	29
3.	Douglas B-18s	30
4.	Martin A-22	30
5.	Northrop A-17	31
6.	North American B-25 "Mitchell"	32
7.	Martin B-26 "Maurader"	32
8.	Douglas O-43	33
9.	North American O-47	34
10.	Curtiss O-52	34

No.	Page
11. Taylorcraft O-57	35
12. Stinson O-49	36
13. Ryan O-51	36
14. Lockheed P-38 "Lightning"	37
15. Bell P-39 "Airacobra"	37
16. Curtiss P-40 "Kittyhawk"	38
17. North American A-36	38
18. Douglas A-24	39
19. Curtiss A-25	39
20. Curtiss C-46 "Commando"	40
21. Douglas C-47 "Gooney Bird"	40
22. Air Superiority	80
23. Interdiction	81
24. Close Air Support	82

Unless otherwise indicated, all illustrations are from U.S. Air Force files.

A PATTERN FOR JOINT OPERATIONS:
WORLD WAR II CLOSE AIR SUPPORT, NORTH AFRICA

PROLOGUE

During World War II (1939-45), as today, close air support had a special notoriety among the many tactical aviation missions. An investigation of events and issues significant to close air support should illustrate its importance in modern warfare, as well as its complex nature that caused great command problems during battlefield operations. Close air support was affected by rapidly changing world events as the nation's military focus shifted from a peacetime to prewar status--a position of cautious defensiveness that involved preparing for a hemisphere defense--and then, in December 1941, from a prewar to wartime status--a position of total offensiveness in Europe and the Far East. Other factors affecting the importance and effectiveness of close air support included the accelerating incidence of mobility, mechanization, and firepower in military operations concepts; the performance of improved aircraft; and the decisions to make greater use of air resources in battle. Close air support issues that captured the greatest attention of the War Department staff and field commanders were usually concerned with identifying aircraft and personnel resources, and their subsequent allocation and control. The latter was especially important in terms of target and mission selection. Most air force leaders felt that air resources could contribute more if used to attack enemy aircraft and ground targets away from the heavily defended battlefield. Most field commanders wanted control of air firepower so that they could mass forces for the ground battle; they wanted close support aviation resources, particularly observation and defensive fighter aircraft, to be considered organic to the battlefield and to be commanded by field commanders. While close air support produced and symbolized a struggle between the air and ground arms of the Army, the senior leaders sought to counterbalance the divisiveness by fostering the idea that subordinate commanders must encourage consensus, cohesion, and cooperation. There were challenges enough just learning to cooperate with the Allies on the ultimate defeat of a determined enemy. Branches of the Army should work toward an effective command front. The problems and compromises that followed indicate that this story of close air support during World War II has a very modern flavor and relevance.

In the late 1930s close air support was meshed into a general category known in the prewar doctrinal manuals as "aviation in support of ground forces."* Tactical aviation, then, included all the specialties that, even today, support the ground forces. Tasks included troop transport, air supply, long-distance reconnaissance, defending against enemy aircraft (especially by maintaining air superiority), and disruption of enemy supply and communications, as well as the tactical tasks associated with close air support. The latter included battlefield observation and liaison, defense of the battlefield and friendly territory from enemy aircraft, and bombing and strafing of enemy forces and weapons in the immediate vicinity of battlefield operations. With a change in the military mission to fit Western Hemisphere defense priorities by 1939, and with the development of faster and bigger aircraft, the War Department modified the concepts for employment of tactical aviation. Close air support, in particular, was devalued in doctrinal statements.

After September 1939, as war ensued in Western Europe, the ground arms of the Army saw a greater need for all kinds of air support and, in thus subsequently stressed their desire for close air support. This happened at a time when the air arm thinking and aviation technology suggested that aircraft operations over the modern battlefield would not be effective or practical. Aircraft were too vulnerable to enemy antiaircraft fire and could not be easily replaced. Close air support became even more marked as a particularly distinctive, troublesome, and complex issue. Even with advancing technology, designing support aircraft proved difficult. Disagreement and debate about doctrine increased; consequently,

---

*The prewar and early war manuals did not use the term "close air support." See Air Corps Field Manual 1-5, Employment of Aviation of the Army, 15 April 1940, which suggested support aviation is poorly suited for direct attacks. "The hostile rear area is the normal zone of action of support aviation. . . ." War Department Training Circular, The Army Air Force--Basic Doctrine, 24 July 1941, declared that operations "in close co-operation with the other arms of the mobile Army" were secondary to interdiction and air superiority missions against invaders of the Western Hemisphere; and War Department Basic Field Manual 31-35, Aviation in Support of the Ground Forces, 9 April 1942, discussed "immediate" and "more distant" targets. Reports from air-ground tests held as early as January 1941 suggested that the airmen and ground force leaders both understood the modern limits and capabilities of close support aviation. They argued among themselves over the implications of a War Department directive that called for compromise and cooperation in modernizing air-ground doctrine.

development of operational procedures stalled in long debates that could not be satisfied in the many field exercises held to test the debated doctrinal ideas. All the while air leaders gained a greater say about aviation matters, both those dealing with support of ground operations and those connected to strategic air warfare operations. Whatever the Army Air Forces mission, its rising influence and growing independence challenged the cohesion of command and pointed to the need for a new consensus among coequal air and ground component commanders.

CHAPTER I

Organization, Doctrine, and Weapons for Close Air Support

The Interwar Years

In the interwar years (1919-38) the United States Army Air Corps considered general air support of ground forces a prime mission function. Air support aviation underwent dramatic changes in these years as airmen and other military and civilian thinkers offered new ideas on the application of air power to warfare. Students and faculty, thinking about air doctrine at the Air Corps Tactical School, Maxwell Field, Alabama, represented the air arm's greatest effort to project aviation into modern warfare. Because of their concern with air support, the scholars at Maxwell outlined battlefield tactics that combined aircraft, tanks, trucks, and mobile field artillery. By 1935 the close air support facet of air support became diffused in a broader, multipurpose conceptualization of air support for the ground, one that included interdiction and air defense roles. The Maxwell scholars began pointing to some revolutionary changes in control of air support aviation: airmen centrally controlling air assets in support of the ground; the air commander not necessarily auxiliary to the ground force commander; and the air force as a full combat arm, coordinate with the Army. With the rise of deadly antiaircraft fire, airmen began to discount their ability to provide close air support.[1]

New mission potentials for aviation, especially coastal defense and long-range bombing tasks, promised further absorption of air support resources. Quite often Air Corps ideas, especially those dealing with independent strategic missions, ran counter to concepts developed at the Army Command and General Staff School at Fort Leavenworth, Kansas, and the Army War College, then in Washington. One idea explored by the airmen at Maxwell and credited to William Mitchell was that bombers alone could stop a naval force. Another, attributed to the famed Italian prophet of the air Giulio Douhet, suggested that fleets of bombers, air power alone, could force an enemy nation to surrender.[2]

As with air arm officers, the ground officers thought about the new mechanization of war. Vigorous debate occurred between air and ground officers, one time in public, as in the Billy Mitchell case. Occasionally the discussion suggested to other branches of the Army that the Air Corps was reluctant about air support in general, not close air support alone. For the most part, ground leaders firmly held to the traditional concept that a ground army was necessary to defeat an enemy force and capture territory; the air arm was primarily an auxiliary force to further the ground force mission. Through the mid-thirties ground officers, having the advantage of tenure, held the leadership mantle in the General Staff and in the field. Although some of these ground staff officers understood the changes in aviation and although some air doctrine that Air Corps leaders regarded as progressive was published, ground-oriented sensibilities controlled the publication of War Department doctrine. Generally, combat arms schools chose not to include even the most elementary new air power thinking in their curriculum, forestalling the education of ground officers at a time when air force roles were gaining importance in military forces worldwide. By the mid-thirties leaders of the Army General Staff, intent on preparing an army for quick mobilization in case of invasion, gave the Air Corps responsibility to organize a combat ready air force. In 1935 the Air Corps organized the General Headquarters (GHQ) Air Force to carry out the function.[3]

In the minds of some ground officers, giving airmen greater command and control authority for a long strike or bombing force only sharpened their desire to control all air functions. But the formation of GHQ Air Force did not include independence comparable to that of the Royal Air Force. GHQ Air Force was subordinate to the Army chief of staff, or his field commander in case of overseas activity.[4] A new training regulation, TR 440-15, Employment of the Air Forces of the Army, 15 October 1935, codified the new Air Corps mission, but also showed how a compromise had been worked out between extreme air and ground views on air arm operational independence. If the air forces might conduct air operations in an independent manner against an invading force before ground armies made contact, TR 440-15 reaffirmed Army doctrine that "air forces further the mission of the territorial or tactical commander to which they are assigned or attached."[5]

More important to understanding the changing concept of close air support, publication of TR 440-15 represented clear concessions to the air doctrine developed over the years at the Air Corps Tactical School. Employment principles discussed in the manual included: emphasis on offensive action, need for central coordination of resources, constant and primary attention to destruction of the enemy's air force, priority for preparation of air forces that would usually precede ground forces into battle, and expectation that air forces would be concentrated against a primary objective "not dispersed or dissipated in minor or secondary operations."[6]

So that the strength of the air forces would not be frittered away, the regulation contained a corollary principle, long promoted by the air forces, cautioning against operations over the battlefield. Enemy troops would be securely fortified and protected against enemy air with effective antiaircraft guns. Ground support operations could be conducted rather in an air defense mode, protecting troops against enemy aircraft. Air operations could interdict concentration of enemy forces, attack communications and ammunition dumps, and harass the enemy's retreat. A primary concern of the ground commanders, to have bombing forces available to attack a dug-in enemy or an enemy artillery piece, was not addressed. Even observation operations in the immediate battle areas were not stipulated in the regulation. That commanders in the field would have to interpret the regulations was clearly intended. The Air Corps' unofficial doctrine had not won full acceptance; but, for the first time, the War Department had opened the door.[7]

In the late thirties the subject of close air support continued to be secondary to more important problems of national war planning. For example, the attention given to the rise of Adolf Hitler's power in Germany and the close association among Germany, Italy, and Japan in 1938 pointed doctrinal thinking towards a different defense concern. War planners feared that an unfriendly foreign power would use Canada or a South American nation as a jumping board to an invasion of the United States. The air arm began to concentrate offensive planning for operations against such an enemy force in the Western Hemisphere. The Air Corps Tactical School instruction increasingly emphasized the importance of long-range bombers, independent strike forces, and industrial targeting.

Air planners worried about close air support aircraft, and directed their concern towards finding an aircraft that would be compatible with modern European war practices. The main experimental attention was given to bigger and faster "attack" types. New models would carry more munitions and have greater speed and defensive armament. This kind of aircraft meant obsolescence of the traditional close support role--flying low and slow to find precise targets, yet still avoiding enemy guns. In the new operational parameters, the latest attack aircraft would not be able to hit the precise targets usually associated with close support aviation. The Air Corps could find no satisfactory airplane type to provide that close-in service desired by the infantry commander on the battlefield.[8]

Increasing Influence of the Air Arm, 1938-1942

In November 1938, concerned about Hitler's bullying of major European nations at Munich to gain the Sudetenland for Germany, and the expansion and quality of European air forces, President Franklin D. Roosevelt opened wide the door to an Army aviation revolution. Whatever the views of the War Department, the president wanted to comply with English and French requests for American aircraft, and he thought by expanding the Air Corps the aircraft industry would produce more for everyone. On the fourteenth he called a group of his military leaders to the White House. Generals Malin Craig, Army chief of staff, George C. Marshall, deputy chief of staff, and Henry H. Arnold, chief of the Air Corps, were among those summoned. The president said he wanted an appropriate force for protection of the Western Hemisphere against the menacing intentions of Germany and Italy. He wanted the Army Air Corps, modernized with the latest combat aircraft, to be that force.[9]

If there was ever an event that changed World War II close air support, this was it. Congress debated the aviation issue for a few months, and then in early 1939 it gave the Air Corps the first in a series of very large budget increases. The presidential and congressional attention helped inflate Air Corps prestige, giving it special rank among the Army combat arms. The new status pointed to prospective independence from a subordinate position in a field army, and fostered a view that air-ground operations would have to be thought of in terms of joint command relations. At the very least, the new influence gave the Air Corps greater leverage to argue its view of ground support aviation as well as other military aviation functions.[10]

The case for the air arm did not develop without counterarguments. For one, the War Department convinced Congress to increase spending for all military forces. In 1939 Congress appropriated large sums for Army expansion and modernization, as well as for aviation. Secondly, with the onset of World War II in September the ground force leaders, impressed by the extensive use of aircraft in the warfare, increasingly desired more aircraft as they updated ground warfare plans. When the part played by the dive bombers in the stunning German Army victories was publicized, the ground arms raised their demand for air support and specialized aircraft for close air support. Diverging viewpoints, strongly expressed, called for concession and accommodation.[11]

General Marshall's leadership did not antagonize the air officers, as did some of his chief of staff predecessors. From the airmen's point of view, Marshall was a true leader of a modern air-ground team. He stood out as a promoter of compromise and cooperation in this time of rapid change in ground and air relationships. He helped institutionalize some differences within the General Staff so that debates were not always publicized as interbranch struggles. Some issues had interbranch proponents and opponents: ground as well as air officers who wanted greater attention given to close air support versus their counterparts who accepted emphasis on interdiction; or advocates for centralized control versus those who wanted air assets controlled at a lower command level.

Marshall understood more about aviation than most ground generals. Over the years he had been a student of air power. In 1938, when he first arrived in Washington, he accompanied Maj. Gen. Frank M. Andrews, then commander of the GHQ Air Force (the operational command of the Air Corps) on a tour of continental air facilities. As deputy chief of staff, in 1939, he and Chief of the Air Corps Arnold, together, "worked out the details of an entire air plan for the War Department."[12] When he assumed chief of staff duties in September 1939, Marshall gave positions on the Army General Staff to large numbers of air officers. As well respected as he was, the appointment of Andrews as assistant chief of staff for operations (G-3), then later as commander of the Panama Defense Command, turned heads among old Army leaders. Andrews became the first air officer to hold the positions normally given to ground officers. Marshall made it a point to appoint staff officers and field commanders who knew about the changes in air warfare.[13]

Working hard to reconcile the differences between air and ground officers, Marshall took the position that the air forces needed to operate with a large degree of autonomy. He validated the functional distinctiveness of and gave great independence to the air forces when he approved an Air Staff for Arnold. In 1940 and 1941 he and Arnold saw eye-to-eye on the long-argued issue of independence for air forces. While many air advocates, in and out of the military, urged independence along the Royal Air Force model, Marshall and Arnold agreed that existing war conditions prevented such a radical reorganization. Still, with the rapid growth of the Army, these leaders understood the need to rely on subordinates, and they gave the staff officers lots of rein and field commanders increased autonomy--supplementary prerogatives of command--especially in operational matters. Arnold kept his word, not advocating an independent organization for the air forces while war continued. It was only natural for him, however, to work consistently for greater influence of the air arm. Technically, Arnold had no command authority over field operations, but found enough flexibility in the wartime Army General Staff and field commands to affect air operations around the world. The rising stock of aviation gave him, and other air leaders, more say in the development of air-ground doctrine.[14]

Requirements for Hemisphere Defense

The German attack on Poland in September 1939 vitalized military thinking about air warfare and particularly sharpened interest in support aviation. The War Department sent officers of all grades and branches to Europe to observe events and send back reports. Concurrent with events in Poland, Harry H. Woodring, the secretary of war, named Arnold to form a board of officers, representing the various Army branches, and to report on the projected employment of an air force. On 1 September the body produced the Air Board Report. Shortly thereafter, Marshall asked for a new statement of air doctrine based on this report. When it was published the following spring, the Air Corps Field Manual (FM) 1-5, Employment of Aviation of the Army, was essentially, like the Air Board Report, a compromise document. It referred to major Air Corps principles, such as the need for air superiority and centralized command. The traditional principle of air warfare as an offensive weapon was not emphasized because war planning was still geared to the likelihood of a Western Hemisphere defense. The function of reconnaissance and liaison air units continued to be that of supporting the ground forces, and the air units retained their permanent assignment under ground force commands. The manual also identified the major air missions for combat or weapons-carrying aircraft under the GHQ Air Force. Along with long-range offensive strikes, air defense against enemy air forces, and miscellaneous patrol and escort functions, the manual listed air support tasks of deep interdiction and "air operations in immediate support of ground forces."[15]

The ground branches' views were also included in FM 1-5. The air forces were clearly divided by specialized function, including specially identified support units, to prevent the GHQ Air Force from overlooking ground support missions as seemed possible with long-range bombardment strike tasks being assigned high priority. The ground officers did not want air units being detached from the GHQ Air Force at the last minute. Rather, they wanted a support aviation force identified as a theater of operations weapon, generally tasked by the higher theater commander. Because in the Western Hemisphere defense war planning ground action was less probable, the ground forces accepted forming a small cadre air support force. This support force would be formed into "a nucleus of aviation especially trained in direct support of ground troops and designated for rapid expansion to meet war requirements. In peacetime this aviation will serve as a small, immediately available force for use in minor emergencies and as a laboratory for the continuous development of methods for its employment."[16]

The Air Corps also gained exposure for its views in this 1940 field manual. FM 1-5 included surprisingly modern air support concepts, some of which would be shelved when the forces organized for the first test of battle in North Africa. For example, a "two-hatted" concept was employed to explain the air leader's simultaneous command of air units and service to the ground commander. "As a commander, he commands all Air Corps troops. . . . As a staff officer, he is the immediate assistant to the (ground) commander and adviser of his staff on all aviation matters." The manual recognized the weakness of aviation in attacking battlefront enemy troops. "Support aviation is not employed against objectives which can be effectively engaged by available ground weapons . . . , [and] aviation is poorly suited for direct attacks against small detachments or troops which are

12

well entrenched or disposed." The manual suggested that the maximum effectiveness of support aviation "is secured through centralized control." Further, "combined operations of air and ground forces must be closely coordinated by the commander of the combined force and all operations conducted in accordance with a well-defined plan." Then, recognizing the constraint of limited air resources, the manual stated that operations in immediate support of ground forces are conducted during the critical phases of combat and prior to and at the conclusion of battle."[17]

Requirements for War With the Axis

Enunciating principles of close air support in April 1940 did not address the complex details and problems of joint air-ground cooperation. The success of Germany's combined arms--first in Poland, then in Western Europe during the spring of 1940--encouraged Congress to support further air force expansion and reorganization and a reevaluation of tactical doctrine. A force in being needed more specific procedures for joint operations than were outlined in FM 1-5. Marshall directed Andrews and his G-3 staff to study the issue anew. In September Andrews issued a memorandum that listed five kinds of air support for ground forces: close air support, air defense of friendly forces and installations, rear area attack, paratroop support, and reconnaissance services. Andrews recommended joint air-ground tests to evaluate the concepts, especially the first two, which required the greatest effort in coordination. After a struggle over timing of exercises, Marshall directed Lt. Gen. Lesley J. McNair, chief of staff of GHQ (a commander's headquarters for all field forces), to conduct a series of exercises.

From 1941 to 1944, as commander of GHQ and Army Ground Forces, McNair was responsible, with Arnold, for joint development of air support, tactical training and doctrine. McNair organized exercises that brought together various air and ground units to experiment with timing and innovative team combinations. More than other Army training or operations officers, he promoted teamwork and cooperation. More than most, he patiently suffered through the continuing teething problems generated by the joining together of the different combat arms. He criticized self-serving attitudes from the air and ground branches. He was especially disturbed by the air force tendency towards independence. He repudiated the view of some air officers that the air arm could win a war by itself, thereby justifying independence. He also opposed division commanders who demanded control of their own air resources, and he relentlessly endorsed the unity-of-command principle.[18]

Marshall also advocated consistently the elementary Army concept that unity of command was paramount for success in battle. Lessons of war suggested to him the need for a unified command structure. He remarked that the German victories in Poland and the Low Countries were founded on "creation of a single high military command for all forces, whether of the land, sea or the air.... In fact the key to the military success of Germany in the present war has not been the operation of the air forces on an independent basis but rather the subordination of air power to the supreme command of the armed forces...."[19]

Arnold believed that strategic bombardment should be a primary ingredient in the battle with the Axis powers, but he too espoused unity of command, although perhaps never with the fervor of a potential field or theater commander, such as McNair and Marshall, and certainly with a different definition of centralized command in the separate arms. Arnold made persistent efforts to satisfy ground force complaints and solve air support problems. As with Marshall and other commanding officers, he had many essential tasks to perform, and close air support was only one of the air facets that crossed his desk. One example of his concern occurred in 1941, when the Army Air Forces was created to give the air forces greater autonomy. Against the advice of staff members, Arnold designated, for the first time in air arm history, a formal advocate for air support. Col. William E. Lynd became the first head of the Air Support Section of the Air Force Combat Command (successor to the GHQ Air Force in June 1941). He could focus attention towards the air-ground team when most needed, just as the rising expectations for war and emphasis in air matters turned towards strategic air warfare.[20]

With the dramatic force expansion in 1941 and reorganizations necessary to improve command and control, Arnold identified a distinct organization for air support. In the new organization the Army Air Forces copied the British idea of numbered air forces "on a Theater of Operations principle," to provide higher-echelon leadership. These air forces would contain specific types of commands, such as bomber commands and fighter commands. The command organization reflected the hope that placing aircraft types together would simplify training, maintenance, and logistics.

The new organization included "air support commands" to "secure the closest type of cooperation with the ground forces."[21] Initially, the air support commands were filled only with air units providing battlefield observation services. Later, in 1942, fighters, dive bombers, and medium and light bombers were placed under the air support command structure to improve air support capability. At GHQ McNair accepted the principles of flexibility and massing of forces, which the air forces stressed; but, with the emergence of mechanized warfare, he worried about specialization in the air and ground arms. He felt that the inclusion of different types of aircraft, as well as the variable unit combinations, added to command confusion.[22] For a number of months McNair was unhappy with formation of the air support commands, which he declared was "one more step in the separation of the air from the rest of the Army."[23]

Lt. Gen. D. C. Emmons, commander of Air Force Combat Command, felt otherwise. He envisioned an air-ground section of a proposed air support command headquarters being physically located with McNair at GHQ. In addition, he proposed that cooperation would be enhanced by locating subordinate air support commands "at airdromes nearest to the headquarters of the forces with which they will work."[24] Further study by the General Staff and the Air Council* confirmed that this organization, with its staff and command, was suitable to overcome the reservations of the ground forces. McNair and air staff officers also agreed that air support service entailed more than just air support command operations and that "all classes of combat aviation of the Army Air Forces must be trained and indoctrinated in performance of the Air Force mission, and in support of the ground and naval forces."[25] The directive that approved the air support commands stated that not only would all aircraft types and units "be trained and used in the support

---

*Formed in March 1941 along with the Army Air Forces, the council's function was to review and coordinate major aviation projects. It consisted of the assistant secretary of war for air, the chief of Army Air Forces, the chief of the War Plans Division of the General Staff, the chief of the Air Corps, the commanding general of the Air Force Combat Command, and others as appointed by the secretary of war.

of ground forces" but that units organic to the air support commands would not "constitute the sole air support of the ground operations."[26]

While the War Department expected the reorganization of the Army Air Forces to improve air-ground cooperation, events pointed to a reduced potential for the close air support facet of air support. In the fall of 1941 the War Department transferred some aviation observation and liaison units and their functions to the operational control of field artillery commands. Only procurement and major maintenance of these units were kept under Army Air Forces responsibility. Not only would the Army Air Forces be less involved in the close air support aspect by transfer of observation units to artillery, but reports from Europe encouraged the Army Air Forces to begin allocating fast fighters and bombers to observation units that they still controlled. The faster aircraft suggested less capability for covering the small-scale, individualized target assignments requested by the ground commanders.

Organization of the theater-echelon air forces--the Twelfth Air Force as an example--and their wide variety of air missions presented a probability of reduced close air support capability. All types of combat commands and all major combat types of aircraft were included in these numbered air forces. How the increased importance of the theater echelon diminished prospects for close air support can be illustrated by Marshall's air policy statement in 1941. In his list of "Basic Principles of Employment of the Air Component of the Army in the Order of Their Priority" close air support ranked fifth in priority out of seven potential missions. Interdiction of enemy armies and air forces, air superiority, and attack on enemy shipping had higher priorities than "close cooperation with other arms of the mobile army. . . ."[27] While Marshall's statement was made with reference to Western Hemisphere defense thinking, the turn to European war planning did not necessarily signify a change in the falling priority of close air support.[28]

Battlefield commanders faced a situation where their supporting air resources were controlled at a higher-echelon command that had different priorities. Control of most air units in a theater was projected as the domain of the theater commanders. This included transports for dropping paratroopers and supplies; observation aircraft to provide theater observation, reconnaissance, and liaison; and the combat bombers and fighters to attack enemy aviation, troop centers, and communication choke points, as well as enemy troops on the immediate front of the ground forces. This left only the air support commands, of uncertain constitution in 1941-42, to be controlled by battlefield commanders.[29]

Air and ground leaders were uneasy at this division of air force resources. For example, the assistant air chief of staff for plans, Brig. Gen. Orvil Anderson, spoke for several leading airmen who felt that any division of the limited and valued air resources weakened the military principle of mass employment. Ground commanders in training argued for larger relative allocation of resources for the air support commands. Now--and throughout the war--Army field commanders and staff officers, in training and combat, complained that the Army Air Forces failed to provide adequate support aircraft.[30]

Testing of these concepts during the series of War Department maneuvers in 1941 was hurt by a shortfall of aircraft and trained squadrons. The maneuver planners, air-ground coordinators, and troop commanders were frustrated when the Army Air Forces did not provide adequate numbers of aircraft for practical testing of air support coordination. McNair also noted that the ground forces failed to employ the limited number of available aircraft realistically. Arnold explained that diverting squadrons from training to the maneuvers would seriously delay training schedules. Ground force planners were not conscious of the requirements of a year-long training program, just for basic pilot instruction. Marshall sided with Arnold but ordered him to compromise and strip some aircraft and personnel from training squadrons. The exercises became more complex through the summer and fall, but ultimately no one was satisfied with the artificiality of aircraft employment, even in the important Louisiana and Carolina maneuvers in late 1941.[31]

As exercise director, McNair now appreciated the necessity for the air and ground forces to emphasize basic instructions within their respective branches in the months ahead. He accepted the idea that pilots had to learn to fly and shoot before training with the ground troops. In December 1941 he and Arnold proposed another series of maneuvers for 1942 to exercise the joint air-ground relationship. The declaration of war abruptly curtailed these plans, as well as many other plans for a smooth buildup of forces.

Air support command structure and concepts for close air support were seriously disrupted throughout 1942.[32] Arnold noted in mid-February that close air support units "are still wallowing around looking for someone who takes an interest in them and in their activities."[33] Even as late as September, when large numbers of forces were committed to combat, Maj. Gen. Jacob L. Devers, commander of armored forces, told Arnold that there was no air-ground support training: "We are simply puttering. Cannot something be done about it?"[34]

By late 1942, as operations captured more firmly the attention of air and ground staff planners and field commanders, a number of problems affected the quality and quantity of air support. Roosevelt showed his support of the Allies by calling for production of large quantities of American aircraft, thereby constricting the flow of airplanes available to air force commands. With war declared, air units were hurriedly concentrated and rearranged. Operational necessities decimated air support and air cooperation demonstration units. For example, the Army Air Forces disbanded the Third Air Support Command to help fill the needs of the newly formed Eighth Air Force to be based in England. The Army Air Forces eliminated the Fifth Air Support Command and redesignated it the Ninth Air Force in April 1942. The War Department removed two of the four air support commands from training and put them into coastal patrol duties to help combat the German submarine offensive against the East and Gulf Coasts.

Marshall, responding to organizational inadequacies revealed by the time of Pearl Harbor, reorganized the General Staff in March 1942. General Headquarters became Army Ground Forces, and both the Army Ground Forces and Army Air Forces gained greater independence of action. The reorganization also raised the level of suspicion between air and ground officers. Ground officers knew that the air force officers eyed jealously the British model for air-ground support. In the Royal Air Force the air units were not attached to ground commanders at any level. The air commander made the decisions on use of air support resources.

Air and ground leaders were also at odds over the air force insistence on training bomber units in strategic and interdiction bombing techniques before training them to support the ground forces. As a result, the Army Air Forces then declared that with time running short, fighter and medium bomber pilots would not receive army support training. The ground arms commands were also suspicious of the name changes given to air units designated to provide close air support (ground-air support command, ground support command, air support command). In turn, some ground commanders asked for the formation of a dedicated ground support air force, fearing that support would not come any other way. In spite of their felt needs, this request suggested a lack of appreciation for the complexities of air operations. It also went in the face of a principle held by some of the staff in Washington that modern ground force units should be more flexible and less encumbered with responsibilities, such as managing air unit operations.[35]

The air forces modified the types of aircraft assigned air support units several times in 1942, adding light bombers and then dive bombers, medium bombers and fighters, giving the ground commander potential access to better ground attack resources. But the problem of giving ground troops realistic air support training continued through the remainder of 1942. In reality, there simply were not enough bases, aircraft, or time as the demands of war overrode expectations of proper training. Even the air representatives at the growing number of ground force schools and training facilities complained about poor air support training exercises because of a deficiency in aircraft numbers.

McNair showed an appreciation of this dilemma, accepting the shortage problem with aircraft and pilots. Arnold agreed that "priority commitments, special diversions, and restricted flow of aircraft to Army Air Forces have prevented [the] fullest desirable allocation of combat aviation for . . . Ground-Air Support training."[36] Somewhat optimistically, Arnold and McNair saw improvements for 1943, but American forces were committed without realistic air-ground training during the confused buildup subsequent to the invasion of North Africa.[37]

Many changes in Army aviation between mid-1940 and mid-1942 affected close air support. Most important was acquisition of a strategic mission to bomb a potential enemy's war-making industry that encouraged greater control of air resources by airmen. A reorganization of air units into air forces similar to European air force models not only precipitated greater centralized control by airmen but also divided attention originally given to close air support and other ground support matters. The airmen compensated by organizing both special air support commands to consolidate units providing close air support for the ground forces and by forming a headquarters staff office dedicated to air support and relations between air and ground arms. Air and ground leaders discussed the meshing of forces in a potential European war scenario and the War Department held exercises to test new theories. With time at a premium in 1942, subsequent to the buildup of forces for operations, the War Department could not insist on realistic air-ground training even if there was a great need for better understanding between air and ground forces.

Doctrine for War

In spite of limitations, planners and commanders used the 1941 maneuvers as the basis, along with observers' reports from Europe, for a final doctrinal statement on air support prior to committing large numbers of American ground forces to combat. As with FM 1-5 in the previous year, the new War Department manual, FM 31-35, Aviation in Support of Ground Forces, published 9 April 1942, was a joint effort, produced by ground and air representatives. By contrast, however, they were more concerned with the organization than with the techniques of air support. They offered no plans for battlefield operations and no priority for targets or missions. Finally, they equivocated about close air support: "Air support targets on the immediate front or flanks of supported units are generally transitory targets of opportunity." In this instance they recommended the dive bomber as the proper aircraft type for close air support, although the air leaders had clearly stated that the dive bomber would be ineffective in close air support where the enemy had good defenses. The manual suggested that deep interdiction targets were the airman's choice.[38]

Neither were the manual writers clear about the sensitive aspects of the command relationship in joint operations (Chart 1). In one aspect they were relatively straightforward: He--that is, the air support commander--was "habitually attached to or supports an army in the theater." Wearing the command hat, he had direct control of all aircraft units, carrying out the general tasking orders from an army or task force commander. Wearing the staff hat, he served as the army staff air support specialist, giving advice and suggestions to the ground arm officers about employment of aircraft in the ground operations. At both levels, command

Chart 1 — Channels of Tactical Control of Combat Aviation in Typified Air Support Command

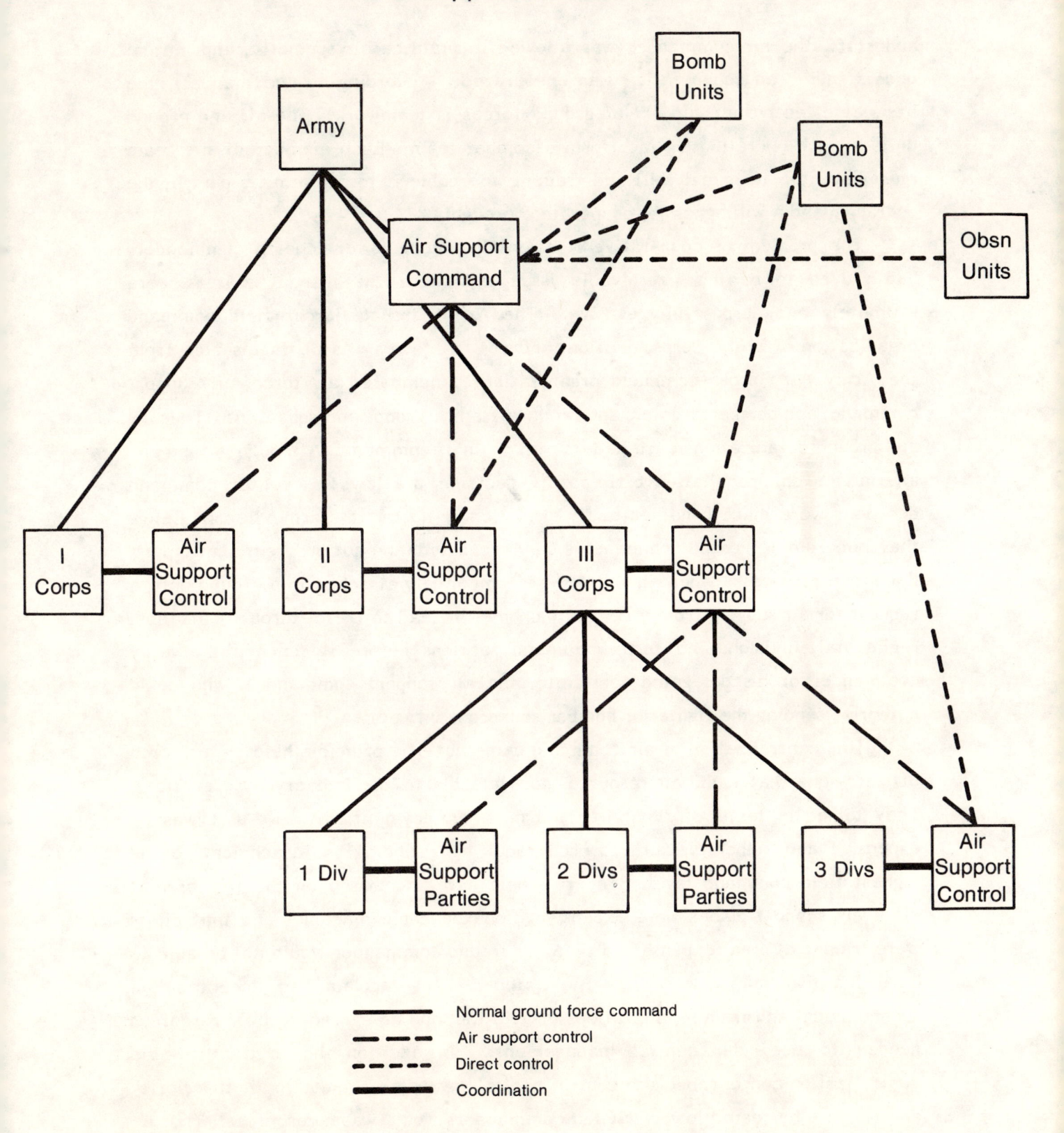

— Normal ground force command
– – – Air support control
- - - Direct control
▬▬ Coordination

Source: War Department Basic Field Manual 31-35, Aviation in Support of Ground Forces, 9 Apr 42, p.4.

and staff, the air commander was allowed to practice his specialty, and mutual understanding and cooperation was encouraged. According to the manual, "the basis of effective air support of ground forces is teamwork. The air and ground units in such operations in fact form a combat team. Each member of the team must have the technical skill and training to enable it to perform its part in the operation and a willingness to cooperate thoroughly."[39]

The problem of cooperative relationship among lower-echelon commanders had proved to be the irresolvable issue, and here the manual writers were ultimately and purposefully evasive. The Army Ground Forces field command organization of army, corps, division, and combat teams was distinguishable from the Army Air Forces command organization of numbered air force, air support command, and bomber, fighter, and reconnaissaince groups and squadrons. Thus air and ground organizations each had its own chain of command. Although ground and air units exchanged liaison officers, by doctrine the lowest level of command decisions were made (whether to fly a mission or not) at the army level. Below that, subordinate ground commanders only requested, and not ordered, air support. Except in rare cases when air units were temporarily attached to a ground unit, a request for air support from a company on the line had to travel through battalion, regimental, division, and corps command sections before it reached the army commander or his delegated substitute, the air support commander, who could authorize sending the fighter or bomber squadrons into action.[40]

This centralization of air command came out of a principle held by air force officers--one that found air resources too valuable to lose in everyday operations. They talked in terms of flexibility and mass employment. An air unit was an expensive and vulnerable air resource requiring rationing by attachment to the highest field command level. The rationale here was based on the reality that close air support planes were expensive, nonexpendable machines and that pilots were trained at great expense and time. A ground commander would not be able to have his own air resources. By October 1941 McNair had accepted the technological and training limitations of aviation, and he agreed that air resources needed to be under central management. In addition, he argued for the centralization concept, because central control was needed to attain air superiority and because he feared lower-echelon commanders would waste resources. Thus he fought against decentralization, favored by the field commanders, even though it promised speedier response time. Indeed, ground commanders perceived the long command and control communications chain in a centralized system as a guarantee of slow air assistance.

Generally, the doctrine acknowledged that the air support commander was an expert in aviation practices and that his airplanes, a scarce resource, would be employed under his direction against the most important target of the ground unit in combat, as decided by the highest ground level commander. In reaction, subordinate field commanders tenaciously expressed dissatisfaction with the idea that an airman at the army staff level had some control over the forces at the corps or division level of battle. Their rationale was the need to ensure "unity of command," wherein all resources, including aircraft, should be under the control of a ground commander. The writers waffled here because they did not really know at what level--division, corps, or army--the ground commander would be during battle. The compromise doctrine, FM 31-35, offered neither true centralization nor unity of command. The air and ground officers who wrote FM 31-35 understood that it was theoretically based, that combat experience was needed to validate doctrine, and that leaders would interpret it in light of specific campaigns.[41]

Additional doctrine published before battle verification in North Africa reflected the expanding importance and increased responsibilities for the air forces. By 1942 there was the greater question of whether any new ideas could be instilled in the minds of field commanders in the midst of preparation for combat. A good example was FM 100-15, Larger Units, issued 29 June 1942. In this document not only was a strategic mission formally established but also a priority was set for one aspect of air support aviation that would restrict efforts at close air support. The manual stated that in campaigns "the initial objective [of air operations] must include the attainment of air superiority." Corps or division commanders accepted the idea of air superiority as a high-priority mission for the air forces, but they expected aircraft for close air support as well. Members of an air support board met in December 1942 to suggest revisions, but the Army Air Forces and Army Ground Forces members argued to delay publication of an updated air support manual until differing concepts were more fully tested in combat.[42]

An additional issue was whether doctrine written by the headquarters staff in 1942 could be disseminated to the field in time to educate and convince regimental, brigade, division, and corps ground commanders, as well as the air commanders of the squadrons, groups, and air commands. The record suggests that indoctrination in air and ground force doctrine tended to be limited to an officer's own arm. Even though it was crucial to close air support operations, neither air nor ground officers gained effective knowledge of each other's branch doctrine until mid-1943, when training programs became more realistic.[43]

Aircraft: Enabling the Execution of Close Air Support

The War Department tackled one other major problem between air and ground, choosing and procuring suitable close air support aircraft, in the prewar period. Limited funding reduced research and development in the interwar years. Then, in 1939, when war preparations opened the purse, the need for operational aircraft was too urgent to start the acquisition process at the basic research level. Lacking many modern aircraft in 1939, the Air Corps now scurried to procure the latest models of all available types. It was forced to rely on the self-initiated design of the aircraft manufacturers. Fortunately, the American aviation industry had been competitive internationally and had done design work on many up-to-date aircraft. The American commercial market and the foreign military market had encouraged research for several years prior to 1939. In particular, the American industries developed radial engines superior to any of European design, and had built superior transport aircraft. In the late thirties, with relatively short development time, the industry modified many of its transport aircraft into light and medium bombers and offered them to foreign and American military organizations.[44]

Design and development of new bombers was one thing; aviation technology was such that engineers could readily produce bigger and faster aircraft. However, aircraft for close support, particularly observation and attack types, had operational requirements that called for characteristics more difficult to produce than size and speed. Aviation engineers in the United States and in foreign countries had failed to find the technology to match those characteristics, and all observation and attack aircraft between 1939 and 1943, American and foreign, were considered obsolete. For aviation technologists, the air battles of 1939 and 1940 in Europe demonstrated that the very latest Air Corps attack and observation models were excessively vulnerable to the speed and guns of fighters and to general ground fire. German light flak (antiaircraft) guns proved so effective that the interwar approach of sneaking into a ground target, flying low and slow between ground obstructions, was no longer possible. In short, the prospect seemed dim for development of an effective weapons-carrying attack plane or observation model for close air support.

Faced with the five-year timelag between design and construction, Arnold was forced to make an important procurement decision in 1939. He started a revolution in attack bombardment doctrine in choosing the Douglas A-20, one of many new light bomber designs offered by the manufacturers, over the more simple, traditional, single engine attack aircraft that could hit small targets identified by the ground commanders. His decision demonstrated the growing popularity of light bomber procurement by European air forces in the immediate months before the invasion of Poland. In doing so, Arnold assumed that the new, larger-sized medium bombers, offered by manufacturers without Air Corps request, might also prove useful for close air support. He expected that these new twin-engined bombers would be fast enough and sufficiently armed to match enemy fighters and that the remarkable speed provided by the new powerful engines would allow aircraft to slip through antiaircraft defenses. Ground force proponents feared that the new bombers were more suited to interdiction bombing and that they would not be capable of hitting targets in close proximity to friendly troops. Maj. Gen. Innis P. Swift, commander of the 1st Cavalry Division in 1942, forwarded a design proposal that was symbolic of the dream of all ground commanders. The proposed aircraft matched all the needs of a weapons-carrying ground support aircraft: long loitering capability, armor protection against ground weapons, and ability to carry a suitable number of weapons and munitions. General Swift understood, however, that success hung on the hope that engineers could develop an engine with suitable horsepower. The Army Air Forces engineers put out bids for such an aircraft, but a prototype was not found until after the war.

Procuring aircraft for the observation role was a more difficult problem than procuring weapons-carrying aircraft, and resulted in years of wrangling between air and ground staff and field proponents. Faced with the problem of the new, fast enemy fighters and the requirement to maintain long loitering capabilities, aircraft designers had an almost impossible technological task. The airmen rejected many designs proposals offered by manufacturers. All proposals compromised speed and defenses, even though most models would have provided good observation platforms in peacetime. Somewhat selfishly, many ground officers felt that observation problems stemmed from the airmen's self-serving concentration on bomber development and that aircraft for close air support observation needs had been neglected.[45]

After months of argument over several types of observation aircraft, in 1941 the ground force planners demanded that a small, lightweight, off-the-shelf, commercial model be procured for battlefield observation duties. The 1941 maneuvers had shown the utility of small aircraft to ground commanders. Some ground officers maintained that the little "Grasshoppers" would be able to observe enemy activities while staying behind friendly lines in their flights. This way they would avoid enemy ground fire. Supporters in the ground forces also believed that the planes' maneuverability would allow them to dodge fighter pursuit. The airmen never fully accepted the light aircraft as a battlefield weapon, but they saw no alternative. Some "standard" observation models, such as the O-47 and O-52 procured for testing between 1939 and 1941, were very fine aircraft in terms of providing good loitering time and good observation for the observers. Yet by 1941 the airmen had determined that they were too vulnerable, by European battlefield standards, both to enemy fighters and ground fire. Instead, the airmen suggested that deep penetration reconnaissance could be carried out by specially modified fighters or fast bombers, and the small planes would be procured until they could find a better close-in observation aircraft.[46]

Understanding many of the problems associated with acquiring suitable close air support aircraft, and usually deferring to the airmen specialists, Marshall in one instance interfered with an Army Air Forces decision. In 1941 he asked the air forces to acquire dive bombers similar to those used by the Germans. The Stuka dive bombers had terrified enemy ground forces by providing precision bombardment of targets close to German troops. Light bombers, using the level-bombing attack mode, could not guarantee pinpoint target destruction. The German dive bomber success captured everyone's attention, and army commanders wanted similar air support. Many argued that this was the only remaining aircraft type that gave field commanders hope for effective weapons-carrying close air support aircraft.[47]

Arnold told Marshall that the Air Corps had tested the dive bomber concept years earlier, rejecting it as dangerous and potentially ineffective because of enemy fighters. He also told Marshall that German dive bombers had been proven too vulnerable in battle, in spite of some success against Poland, France, and the Soviet Union. The Germans had, in fact, comprehended the weakness of the type and did not intend to employ the dive bombers in theaters where their enemy had first-line fighters. Nonetheless, probably overly sensitive to the complaints of ground forces and wanting to provide a surrogate, Marshall insisted. Arnold complied by ordering the acquisition of dive bombers for the air support commands. Because the Army Air Forces had neither dive bombers nor any in design, the air staff ordered quantities of modified Navy models and had the first production P-51 fighters modified with dive brakes and wing racks to fill the requirement.

In 1940 and 1941 the identification of aircraft for close air support tasks held the attention of both air and ground leaders. However, by 1942, they knew that the performance of thier forces really would be tested in cooperative--joint--operations of close air support. Limited time prevented careful study of operational problems and weaknesses. A war-experienced Royal Air Force group captain visiting the War Department predicted some possible problems with the American air support system, especially with planning. He foresaw that Americans would have to undertake more intensive planning and develop a permanent staff to coordinate all the services and arms cooperating in air support. He suggested that planners needed to recognize how quickly air forces were wasted away in battle conditions. Maj. Gen. George C. Kenney, commanding the Fourth Air Force in San Francisco, in April 1942, also offered some predictive observations. He warned that air support would take lots of planes, for observation, attack, and top cover. Any stinginess and the system would fail.[48]

Some offices of the War Department made note of Kenney's admonitions, but the preparation for an attack against the Nazis in Europe, as well as other theater activities, engrossed much of the staff effort and consumed the attention of field commanders desperately preparing their minimally trained troops for overseas passage. By late 1942 the War Department had assigned the expanding air forces many functions. Close air support of ground forces was but one troublesome aspect of air power. Still, the ground leaders saw a great need for aircraft in the battle against Axis powers, and they got assurance from the War Department that they would have the air support commands dedicated to support the ground battle. They also won the promise of potential support from fighter and bomber commands. War Department leaders generally agreed on doctrine for joint arms warfare, written in light of European war experiences, although there were questions about command of forces at lower levels and about the indoctrination of field commanders. Arnold admitted freely that the air forces were only partially trained. He foresaw problems with close air support, as well as other facets of military activity, in forthcoming operations in North Africa.[49]

Some of the attack aircraft supporting the ground forces in the late thirties were revolutionary in size, speed, and bomb-carrying capacity. Portrayed are Curtiss A-18s (*top*) flying low in the attack mode and the popular Douglas A-20 (*bottom*), first acquired in 1939 and used throughout the war.

Several twin-engined tactical bombers, modified from commerical transport aircraft, were offered by the alert aircraft industry in the late thirties. Portrayed are Douglas B-18s (*top*), shown here flying in formation over California, and a Martin A-22 (*bottom*) on the ramp.

A more conventional attack aircraft, the Northrop A-17, last of the prewar single-engine attack airplanes, was a successful flyer and was much faster than its predecessors. A-17s were procured in great quantity between 1936 and 1941, but after the United States became involved in the war, it was clear to all that this aircraft would be inadequate in speed, range, and bomb-carrying capability.

The Army Air Forces acquired two medium bombers beginning in 1941, the North American B-25 "Mitchell" (*top*) and the Martin B-26 "Maurader" (*bottom*), with the expectation of providing the ground forces additional close air support as well as interdiction and strike missions.

The Air Corps bought dozens of different observation-type aircraft in the late thirties. Some were modified from pursuit or attack aircraft types. Several, like this Douglas O-43, were good observation platforms, but the increasingly fast fighter aircraft beginning to fly in foreign air forces suggested that conventional observation aircraft would be extremely vulnerable.

Then in the late thirties the Air Corps sought a more powerful, faster, all-metal monoplane type for observation tasks. The North American O-47 (*top*) and Curtiss O-52 (*bottom*) were excellent flyers. The O-47 had an observation bay below the wing; the O-52 used a high-wing configuration to allow the flight crew an unobstructed view below.

The most popular observation aircraft of the war were the light "Grasshoppers," like this Taylorcraft O-57. With only a 65-horsepower engine and simple construction, they were inexpensive and easy to operate and maintain, but they could only operate behind friendly lines or when the skies were clear of enemy fighters.

In addition, the Air Corps procured a number of light aircraft, basically modified from commercial sports planes, to give the ground forces close air support service once air superiority had been gained. Some of the models were highly maneuverable and performed well at slow speeds. The Stinson O-49 (*top*) was a successful model used throughout the war. The Ryan O-51 (*bottom*) had high-lift wings that permitted operations in and out of small fields.

To complement the light observation aircraft, airmen turned to modified fighters for the needed observation over enemy lines. Once the lessons of battle came in, they also modified these planes with bomb racks and operated them in close air support missions. Portrayed are two of the fighter aircraft types of World War II that were modified into fighter-bombers, the Lockheed P-38 "Lightning" (*top*) and the Bell P-39 "Airacobra" (*bottom*).

The Curtiss P-40 "Kittyhawk" (*top*) and the North American A-36 (*bottom*) did yeoman close air support service in North Africa and in the Mediterranean Theater.

Neither the A-36 nor other dive bombers, such as the Douglas A-24 (*top*) and the Curtiss A-25 (*bottom*), were successful in battle, which finally led to their withdrawal in favor of fighter-bombers.

Before 1940 the Air Corps had many varieties of cargo transports to serve its own operational flying squadrons. The famous Curtiss C-46 "Commando" (*top*) and the Douglas C-47 "Gooney Bird" (*bottom*) were acquired in large numbers to meet the expanding requirements of all services. In close air support tasks these aircraft provided the ground forces with both cargo and personnel airborne transport.

Endnotes—Chapter I

1. Thomas H. Greer, The Development of Air Doctrine in the Army Air Army, 1917-1941, USAF Historical Studies no. 89 (Maxwell Air Force Base: USAF Historical Division, Research Studies Institute, Air University, 1955), pp. 40-41.

2. Oral Interv no. 729, Gen Earle E. Partridge, April 1974, pp. 60-68 and 221-27 (Partridge claimed that there was a balanced curriculum at the Air Corps Tactical School and that the air forces were organized for cooperation with the Army ground forces), USAF Historical Research Center (USAFHRC) Oral History Collection, Maxwell Air Force Base (MAFB); Maj Gen Orvil A. Anderson, "Development of US Strategic Air Doctrine, ETO WW II" (Speech delivered at Air War College, September 20, 1951), USAFHRC Microfilm Collection, 239.71651-9, MAFB.

3. Greer, Air Doctrine, pp. 44-106. See also Oral Intervs no. 729, Partridge, April 1974, and no. 898, Maj Gen Orvil A. Anderson, October 1959, USAFHRC Oral History Collection, MAFB; R. Earl McClendon, The Question of Autonomy for the U.S. Air Army, 1907-1945 (Maxwell Air Force Base: Documentary Research Division, Air University, 1954), pp. 151-52; John F. Shiner, Foulois and the U.S. Army Air Corps, 1931-1935 (Washington, D.C.: Office of Air Force History, 1983), pp. 43-255.

4. McClendon, Question of Autonomy, pp. 151-52.

5. Robert Frank Futrell, Ideas, Concepts, Doctrine: A History of Basic Thinking in the United States Air Force (Maxwell Air Force Base: Air University, 1974), pp. 40-41.

6. War Department Training Regulation 440-15, Air Corps, Employment of the Air Forces of the Army, 15 Oct 35.

7. Ibid.

8. Greer, Air Doctrine, pp. 76-83 and 87-88. See also William A. Jacobs, "Tactical Air Doctrine and AAF Close Air Support in the European Theater, 1944-1945," Aerospace Historian, March 1980, pp. 35-49.

9. Mark Skinner Watson, Chief of Staff: Prewar Plans and Preparations. United States Army in World War II (Washington, D.C.: Historical Division, U.S. Army, 1950), pp. 132-46.

10. Wesley Frank Craven and James Lea Cate, eds., The Army Air Forces in World War II, 7 vols. (Chicago: University of Chicago Press, 1948-58), vol. 1, Plans and Early Operations, January 1939 to August 1942 (1948), p. 104; Futrell, Ideas, p. 49; H. H. Arnold, Global Mission (New York: Harper, 1949), pp. 177-80.

11. Craven and Cate, Plans and Early Operations, 1:104; Arnold, Global Mission, pp. 177-80; Maj Gen L. S. Kuter, "Organization of Top Echelons in World War II" (Lecture delivered at War College, February 28, 1949), pp. 2-6 (hereafter cited as Kuter Lecture), USAFHRC Microfilm Collection, MAFB.

12. Arnold, Global Mission, p. 180.

13. Watson, Chief of Staff, pp. 77, 152-55, 162-78, Dewitt S. Copp, A Few Great Captains (Garden City, N.J.: Doubleday, 1980), pp. 428 and 434-37; George Catlett Marshall, The Papers of George Catlett Marshall, ed. Larry I. Bland (Baltimore: John Hopkins Press, 1981--), vol. 1, The Soldierly Spirit, December 1880-June 1939 (1981), pp. 611, 617, 618, 620-24; Forrest C. Pogue, George C. Marshall (New York: Viking, 1963-87), vol. 2, Ordeal and Hope, 1939-1942 (1965), pp. 48-50 and 82-85; Harold B. Hinton, Air Victory: The Men and Machines, (New York: Harper, 1948), p. 87; Arnold, Global Mission, p. 179; Memo, Gen Malin Craig, CofS, WD, to Asst CofS, G-2, WD, 17 Mar 39, file OCS 14100-21, RG 165, National Archives and Records Administration (NARA); Memo, Craig to Asst CofS, G-2, WD, 24 May 38, file OCS 14110-23, RG 165, NARA; Kuter Lecture, pp. 2-6.

14. Ltr, Maj Gen H. H. Arnold, Chief, Air Corps, to Karl H. Von Weigand, Foreign Service Editor, International New Service, 6 Mar 39, file 381, CDF 1939-1942, RG 18, NARA; Arnold, Global Mission, pp. 179-83; Futrell, Ideas, pp. 48-49; Marshall, Papers of George Catlett Marshall, 1:631-35; Copp, A Few Great Captains, pp. 448-49; Watson, Chief of Staff, pp. 280-86.

15. Quoted words from Air Corps Field Manual 1-5, Employment of Aviation of 15 Apr 40. See also Greer, Air Doctrine, pp. 112-15; Futrell, Ideas, p. 51.

16. Air Corps Field Manual 1-5, Employment of Aviation of the Army, 15 Apr 40.

17. Ibid.

18. Kent Roberts Greenfield, Robert R. Palmer, and Bell I. Wiley, The Organization of Ground Combat Troops, United States Army in World War II (Washington, D.C.: Historical Division, U.S. Army, 1947), pp. 99-107, 115-18, 134-39.

19. Watson, Chief of Staff, p. 294.

20. Arnold, Global Mission, pp. 181-99; See Air Support Directorate, HQAAF/AFRAS documents in files 373.21, AAF, CDF 1942-1944 and 321.9, CDF 1939-1942, RG 18, NARA. See also records in USAFHRC Microfilm Collection, 143.04-4, MAFB; Memo, Maj Gen George H. Brett, Chief, Air Corps, to Asst CofS, WPD, WD, 5 Jun 41, sub: Air Force Requirements, files 452.1, "F" Airplanes Reports, Entry 293, Series II, CDF 1939-1942, RG 18, NARA; Greenfield et al., Organization of Ground Combat Troops, pp. 99-101; Watson, Chief of Staff, pp. 284-95; Pogue, Ordeal and Hope, 2: 83-86.

21. Frank Robert Futrell, Command of Observation Aviation: A Study in Control of Tactical Airpower, USAF Historical Study no. 24 (Maxwell Air Force Base: USAF Historical Division, 1956), p. 12.

22. Ibid., pp. 1-21; Greenfield et al., Organization of Ground Combat Troops, p. 108; Memo, Lt Gen Delos C. Emmons, Cdr, HQ, Air Force Combat Command (AFCC), to Chief, Army Air Forces (AAF), 3 Jul 41, USAFHRC Microfilm Collection, 322.082, MAFB; Craven and Cate, Plans and Early Operations, 1: 144 and 158-59; Wesley Frank Craven and James Lea Cate, eds., The Army Air Forces in World War II, 7 vols. (Chicago: University of Chicago Press, 1948-58), vol. 6, Men and Planes (1955), pp. 52-55; "Cooperative Aviation: Five Support Commands," The Air Corps News Letter, August 1941, pp. 1, 4, 30; Memo, George C. Marshall, CofS, WD, to Chief, Air Corps, 22 Jul 41, USAFHRC Microfilm Collection, 145.96-63, MAFB; Ltr, Adjutant General, WD, to Chief, AAF, 25 Jul 42, sub: Air Support Aviation, file 381, CDF 1939-1942, RG 18, NARA; Minutes of Initial Meeting of Air Council, 2 Jul 41, War Department, file 334.8, CDF 1939-1942, RG 18, NARA.

23. Kent Roberts Greenfield, Army Ground Forces and the Air-Ground Battle Team, Including Organic Light Aviation, U.S. Army Study no. 35 (Washington, D.C.: Historical Section, Army Ground Forces, 1948), p. 7.

24. Futrell, Command of Observation Aviation, p. 12.

25. Ibid.

26. Directive, Adjutant General, WD, to Chief, AAF, 25 Jul 41. sub: Air Support Aviation, file 381, CDF 1939-1942, RG 18, NARA; Herman S. Wolk, Planning and Organizing the Postwar Air Force, 1943-1947 (Washington, D.C.: Office of Air Force History, 1984), pp. 21-22.

27. Memo for Chief of AAF (probably sent by Maj Gen Carl Spaatz, Asst CofS, AAF), 22 Jul 41, USAFHRC Microfilm Collection, 145.96-63, MAFB.

28. Craven and Cate, Plans and Early Operations, 1:586-88; Memo, Col H. L. George, Asst Air Chief of Staff, A-WPD, WD, to CofS, WD, 18 Feb 42, sub: Readjustment of Air Support Organizations, USAFHRC Microfilm Collection, 145.96-63, MAFB; Memo, Col William E. Lynd, Director, Air Support, AFCC, to CofS, AAF, 3 Feb 42, sub: Organization of Air Support, file 321.9, CDF 1939-1942, NARA; Memo, Col John Y. York, Jr., to Asst CofS, A-3, WD, 31 Mar 42, sub: Status of 5th Ground Support Command, file 321.9, CDF 1939-1942, RG 18 NARA; 1st End, CG, Air Force Technical Training Command, Knollwood Field, N.C., 4 Jul 42, sub: Ground-Air Support Command, to Memo, Col D. M. Schlatter, Director, Ground-Air Support, WD, 4 July 42, same sub, file 321.9, CDF 1939-1942, RG 18, NARA; Memo, Col B. E. Gates, Director, Management Control, WD, to Director, Military Requirements, WD, 14 Jul 42, sub: Transfer of Functional Responsibility for Light and Dive Bombardment . . . , file 452.1, CDF 1939-1942, RG 18, NARA; Memo (for

oral presentation), Brig Gen T. J. Hanley, Jr., to Arnold, 5 Nov 42, sub: Air Support for Ground Forces, file 373.21, AAF CDF, Oct 1942 to May 1944, RG 18, NARA; Ltr (and attachments), Maj Gen George C. Kenney, Cdr, Fourth Air Force, to Lt Gen H. H. Arnold, Cdr, AAF, 25 Apr 42, file 385C, CDF 1939-1942, RG 18, NARA.

29. Greenfield, Army Ground Forces and the Air-Ground Battle Team, p. 7.

30. Futrell, Ideas, pp. 77-78.

31. Memo, Emmons, Cdr, HQ, AFCC, to Chief, AAF, 8 Oct 41, file Chief of AAF, Entry 241a, RG 18, NARA; Memo (and attached staff sheet), Arnold to Asst SecWar John J. McCloy, 15 Mar 42, H. H. Arnold Manuscript Collection, box 44, Library of Congress (LOC); Greenfield et al., Organization of Ground Troops, pp. 104-08.

32. Greenfield, Army Ground Forces and the Air-Ground Battle Team, pp. 7-9 and 29-44; Memo, Lynd, Director, Air Support, AFCC, to CofS, WD and AAF, 3 Feb 42, sub: Organization of Air Support, file 321.9, CDF 1939-1942, RG 18, NARA.

33. Memo, Schlatter, Office of Director of Ground-Air Support, WD, to Director, Military Requirements, WD, 20 Apr 42, sub: Comments of General Brereton's Cablegram; Memo, Arnold to Schlatter, 14 Mar 42, sub: Needs and Requirements of Our Observation Squadrons and Support Units. Both in H. H. Arnold Manuscript Collection, box 44, LOC.

34. Ltr, Maj Gen Jacob L. Devers, Cdr, HQ, Armored Forces, Fort Knox, Ky., to Arnold, 5 Sep 42, H. H. Arnold Manuscript Collection, box 44, LOC.

35. Ibid.; Memo, Spaatz, Cdr, HQ, AFCC, to Chief, AAF, 2 Mar 42, sub: Organization of Air Support, file 321.9, CDF 1939-1942, RG 18, NARA; Directive, P. M. Whitney, Asst Adjutant General, WD, to CG, HQ, AFCC, 21 Feb 42, sub: Organization of Air Support, file 321.9, CDF 1939-1942, RG 18, NARA; Routing and Record Sheet, HQ, AAF, AFROM to AFACT, 4 Mar 42, sub: Status of 5th Ground Support Command, file 321.9, CDF 1939-1942, RG 18, NARA; Routing and Record Sheet, HQ, AAF, AFDAS to AFRGS, Kuter to Schlatter, 1 May 42, USAFHRC Microfilm Collection, 145.96-54, MAFB; Ltr, Brig Gen John B. Brooks, Cdr, HQ, II Air Support Command, to Arnold and Schlatter via Second Air Force, 20 Nov 42, file 373.21, CDF Oct 1942 to May 1944, RG 18, NARA; Routing and Records Sheet, HQ, AAF, 11 Apr 42, sub: Air-Ground Cooperative Training, with attached AFRGS (AAF Ground Support Directorate) Rpt, 14 Apr 42, file 353 F, CDF 1939-1942, RG 18, NARA; Memo, Gates, Director, Management Control, WD, to Director, Military Requirements, WD, 14 Jul 42, sub: Transfer of Functional Responsibility for Light and Dive Bombardment Aviation . . . , 14 Jul 42, file 452.1, CDF 1939-1942, RG 18, NARA.

36. Memo, Arnold to CofS, WD, 20 Jul 42, sub: Ground-Air Support of Armored Forces, H. H. Arnold Manuscript Collection, box 42, LOC.

37. Memo, Arnold to SecWar, 23 Oct 42, sub: Aviation in Support of the Army Ground Forces, H. H. Arnold Manuscript Collection, box 42, LOC.

38. Quoted words from War Department Basic Field Manual 31-35, Aviation in Support of Ground Forces, 9 Apr 42. See also Greenfield et al., Organization of Ground Troops, pp. 110-14.

39. Quoted words from War Department Basic Field Manual 31-35, Aviation in Support of Ground Forces, 9 Apr 42. See also Schlatter to CGs, Second and Third Air Forces, 3 Jun 42, sub: Reorganization of Observation Aviation, file 321.9, CDF 1939-1942, RG 18, NARA.

40. Greenfield et al., Organization of Ground Troops, p. 112.

41. War Department Field Manual 31-35, Aviation in Support of Ground Forces, 9 Apr 42; Greenfield et al., Organization of Ground Troops, pp. 110-14.

42. Quoted words from War Department Field Service Regulation, FM 100-15, Larger Units, 29 Jun 42. See also Futrell, Ideas, p. 66.

43. Memo, Arnold to CofS, WD, 20 Jul 42, sub: Ground-Air Support of Armored Forces; Memo, Arnold to SecWar, 23 Oct 42, sub: Aviation in Support of the Army Ground Forces. Both in H. H. Arnold Manuscript Collection, box 42, LOC.

44. Futrell, Ideas, pp. 49-51; Stetson Conn and Byron Fairchild, The Framework of Hemisphere Defense, United States Army in World War II (Washington, D.C., Office of Chief of Military History, U.S. Army, 1960), pp 16-19; Final Report of the Air Corps Board on Revision to the 5-year Experimental Program, 23 Jun 39, in Lyons Records (large indexed microfilm collection), Historians Office, Wright-Patterson Air Force Base (WPAFB); Ltr, Adjutant General, WD, to Chief, Air Corps, 30 Oct 39, sub: Airplane Replacement and Research and Development Programs, Lyons Records, WPAFB.

45. J. V. Mizrahi, Air Corps (Northridge, Calif.: Sentry Books, 1970), pp. 99-103; Memo, Sherman Miles, Acting Asst CofS, G-2, WD, to Asst CofS, WPD, WD, 6 Jul 40, sub: Foreign Air Doctrine, Lyons Records, WPAFB; Memo, Brig Gen George H. Brett, Chief, Material Division, WD, to Chief, Air Corps, 31 May 39, Lyons Records, WPAFB; Rpt, 10 May 39, sub: Board of Officers Convened To Appraise Attack Bomber Designs . . . , file 452.1 "A" Attack Bombers, Classified CDF 1939-1942, Entry 293, RG 18, NARA; Ltr, Arnold to President, Air Corps Board, MAFB, 18 Aug 37, USAFHRC Microfilm Collection, 145.93-117, MAFB; Ltr, Arnold to Asst SecWar, 10 Jan 39, sub: Prototype Attack Bomber Airplane, Lyons Records, WPAFB; News Bulletin, Leonard H. Engel, "Army To Select Prototype For New Class Of Plane in Wright Field Competition; Attack Bomber Will Replace Attack Plane If Successful," 24 Jan 39, file 452.1, CDF 1939-1942, RG 18, NARA; Memo to Air Corps Board, sub: Study no. 35, USAFHRC Microfilm Collection, 248-22-25, MAFB; Rpt, 3 Jul 42, sub: Use of Aircraft for Anti-tank Defense, file 381 B, CDF 1939-1942, RG 18, NARA.

46. Robert J. Waag, "Spy in the Sky," <u>Air Power</u>, January 1975, pp. 30-43; Futrell, <u>Command of Observation Aviation</u>, pp. 1-11; Rick Glasebrook, "Flying the North American O-47 and the Curtiss-Wright O-52," <u>Aerospace Historian</u>, March 1978, pp. 5-11; Craven and Cate, <u>Plans and Early Operations</u>, 1:618-21; Ltr, Arnold to Adjutant General, WD, 9 May 39, sub: Military Characteristics of Aircraft, file 452.1 "A," Entry 293, Series II, Classified CDF 1939-1942, RG 18, NARA; Proceedings of a Board of Officers Appointed by the Following Orders, 16 May 39, approved by Arnold, headed by Col Clarence L. Tinker, file 452.1 "B," Entry 293, Series II, Classified CDF 1939-1942, RG 18, NARA; Memo, Arnold to Tinker, 10 May 39 (Arnold started the search for a slow speed liaison plane early in 1939), file 452.1-H Observation Planes, CDF 1939-1942, RG 18, NARA; Mal Holcomb, "Send Grasshoppers!: How the U.S. Army Air Corps Procured a Fleet of Liaison/Observation Aircraft Almost Overnight, in Spite of Itself," <u>Wings</u>, February 1983, pp. 40-49; Irving B. Holley, Jr., <u>Evolution of the Liaison-type Airplane, 1917-1944</u> (Washington, D.C.: AAF Historical Office, 1946).

47. Memo, Robert A. Lovett, Asst SecWar for Air, to Chief, AAF, 14 Aug 41, sub: Procurement Service Quantity of Light Commercial Type Airplanes; Ltr, Lt Gen J. L. DeWitt, Cdr, Fourth Army, to Marshall, 5 Aug 41; Rpt, Col Robert E. M. Goolrick, Cdr, Air Corps Troops, IX Army Corps, to CG, IX Army Corps, Fort Lewis, Wash., 17 Mar 41, sub: Observation With the Corps. All in USAFHRC Microfilm Collection, 248.2208B, MAFB.

48. Waag, "Spy in the Sky," pp. 30-43; Futrell, <u>Command of Observation Aviation</u>, pp. 1-11; Glasebrook, "Flying the North American O-47 and the Curtiss-Wright O-52," pp. 5-11; Ltr, Arnold to Adjutant General, WD, 9 May 39, sub: Military Characteristics of Aircraft, file 452.1 "A," Entry 293, Series II, Classified CDF 1939-1942, RG 18, NARA; Proceedings of a Board of Officers Appointed by the Following Orders, 16 May 39, approved by Arnold, headed by Col Clarence L. Tinker, file 452.1 "B," Entry 293, Series II, Classified CDF 1939-1942, RG 18, NARA; Memo, Arnold to Tinker, 10 May 39, file 452.1-H Observation Planes, CDF 1939-1942, RG 18, NARA; Holcomb, "Send Grasshoppers!," pp. 40-49; Holley, <u>Evolution of the Liaison-type Airplane, 1917-1944</u>; Ltr, Kenney to Arnold, 25 Apr 42, and attached report, "Air Support of Task Force Offensive Operations," file 385C, CDF 1939-1942, RG 18, NARA; Memo, Lynd, Air Support Section, AFCC, to CG, AFCC, 3 Feb 42, sub: Summary of Items Discussed at Informal Conference, Group Captain Willet, RAF . . . , file 385C, CDF 1939-1942, RG 18, NARA..

49. Memo, Arnold to Schlatter, 23 Dec 42, sub: Teamwork Between Air and Ground Units, H. H. Arnold Manuscript Collection, box 42, LOC.

CHAPTER II

North African Close Air Support Operations

World War II Operations and North Africa

Intelligence sources did not anticipate the Japanese attack on Pearl Harbor that brought the United States into war. Despite the buildup of forces and planning for potential war during 1939 and 1940, the War Department was not as prepared as it wanted to be. Still, the military flung what it had into battle with the Japanese and began a buildup of forces in Europe and other parts of the world. Marshall recognized that it would require months before a ground force could be raised big enough for an invasion of the Continent. The British believed it would take years. Army Air Forces leaders promised that their forces could start an offensive against the Germans earlier than the ground forces, but it meant a slowdown in development of air support forces. With presidential approval, in early 1942, the Eighth Air Force started preparations for a bombing campaign against Germany.

Then in mid-1942, pressured by the Russians and British to start a serious land offensive, Roosevelt insisted that the military follow the British suggestion and initiate a ground and air campaign in North Africa before the end of the year. Field General Erwin Rommel's June offensive had created a crisis for the British in the desert west of Cairo. In response, the Americans lined up some air units, initiating the process with a detachment of B-24s under Col. Harry A. Halverson. By the fall of 1942 the United States had sent a sizable American contingent of aircraft to the British Western Desert Air Force, including some assigned to close air support roles (Map 1). By November American forces had formed into the Ninth Air Force, commanded by Maj. Gen. L. H. Brereton.

American aviators gained experience with the unique British air-ground cooperation system for the first time. The combined forces of General Sir Bernard L. Montgomery's Eighth Army and the air units of Air Vice Marshal Sir Arthur Coningham's Western Desert Air Force shared a great victory between August and October 1942 in the desert west of Cairo. Montgomery and Coningham mutually decided that ground and aviation command components functioned best as equal partners at the army level. Air and ground field staffs also had the same headquarters and living quarters. It was a true joint command, as neither

47

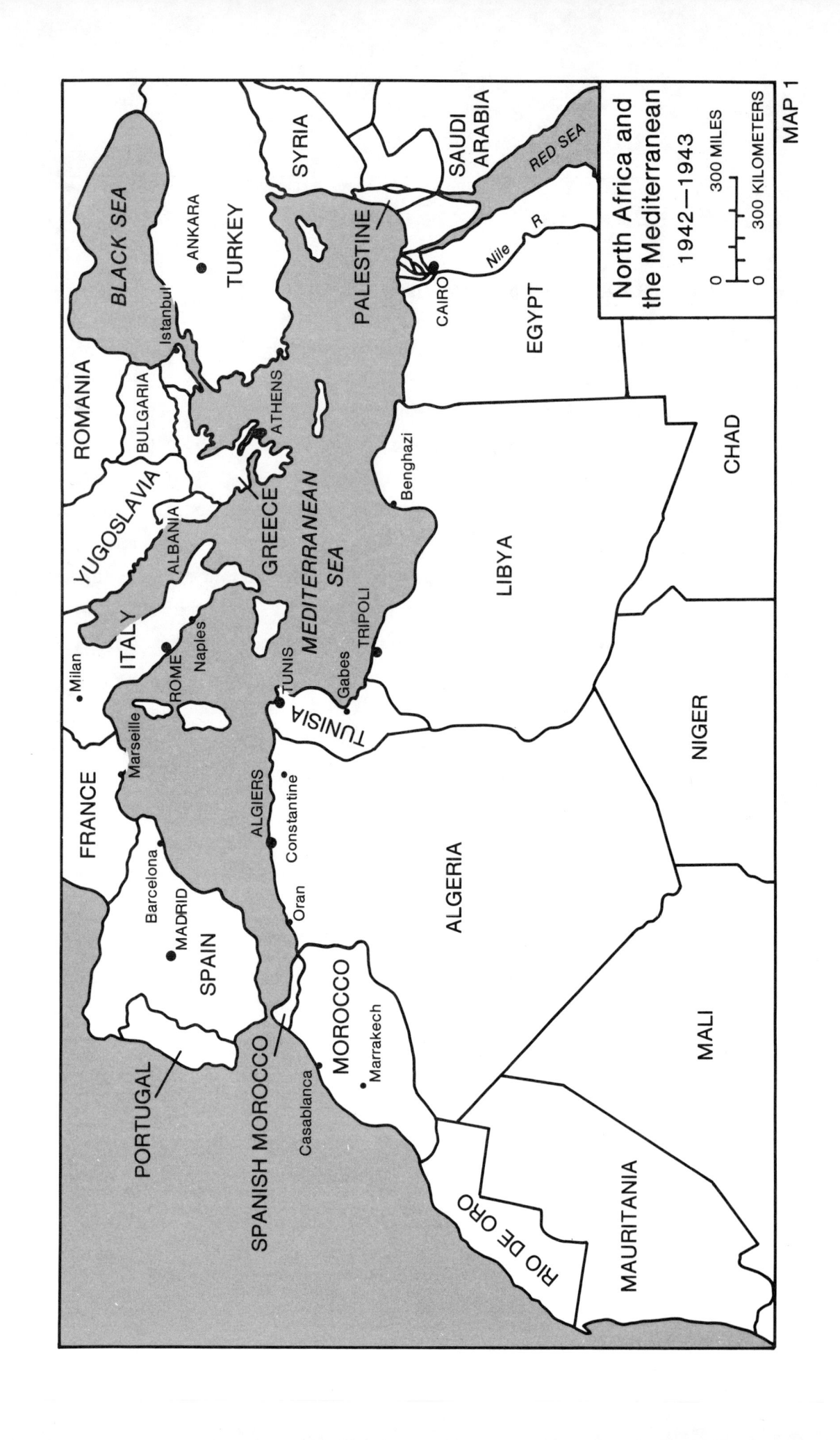

MAP 1. North Africa and the Mediterranean 1942–1943

Montgomery nor Coningham demanded final authority. It helped that the techniques involved in joint command were amenable to offensive, as opposed to defensive, operations. Success in pushing Rommel to the west helped make the adventure a positive one in the minds of many observers and participants. By August Brereton had grasped the significance of Coningham's employment of air support fighters and bombers. He reported to Arnold on the importance of the command arrangement in the Western Desert, and how the cooperation came from a natural sympathy and understanding between air and ground commander.[1]

At the same time, as staff and forces were gathering in England for Operation TORCH, Allied strategists were contending with multiplying demands for resources from other theaters. Increasing requirements for worldwide operations reduced air resources for close air support. The fight against Rommel to clear the Mediterranean received special attention, if not a higher priority than TORCH, in the late summer of 1942. The desire to relieve pressure against the Soviet Union grew in importance as the victorious German summer campaign brought the Axis into the Caucasus and closer to the Middle East. The Allies juggled resources to expand the commitment to the Middle East. Thus, large quantities of fighters and light and medium bombers, used in close support work, were diverted from TORCH to the Western Desert, the Middle East, and Russia. In one case, General Dwight David Eisenhower, supreme commander of TORCH, interceded to prevent the 33d Fighter Group from being sent to the Western Desert.[2]

On 2 October President Roosevelt directed Secretary of War Henry L. Stimson to increase the flow of aircraft to Russia. Marshall was concerned, and after conferences with Arnold and presidential adviser Harry Hopkins, he went directly to the president. He told Roosevelt that the only way to increase the monthly lend-lease airplane schedule to the Soviet Union would be "a reduction of planes urgently needed for our units in combat theaters, or to curtail seriously the plans for TORCH. Roosevelt wanted TORCH to be a success, but he kept pressure on Marshall to support all theaters. For example, on 24 October Roosevelt ordered his military chiefs to make sure the South Pacific as well as North Africa operations were supported with "munitions and planes and crews. . . ." In order "to take advantage of our success, "he judged, "we must have adequate air support in both places...." In England, planning for the invasion of North Africa, Eisenhower wanted as much air power as possible. He was not entirely clear about the published doctrine on close air support, and he was uncertain about understanding among his lieutenants. He would give close air support special attention. After all this was the first major land campaign for the United States, and the eyes of the Americans and Allies were looking for results.[3]

Planning Close Air Support for North Africa

In October 1942, just weeks before the landing in North Africa, Eisenhower's Allied Force Headquarters (AFHQ) planners issued an operations memorandum on the subject of close air support. In this directive, "Combat Aviation in Direct Support* of Ground Units," the planners attempted to clarify command and control authority and to prescribe methods of coordinating the air units in direct support of ground forces. They noted that American and British doctrine agreed, pointing out that the basic American FM 31-35 matched British Army Training Instruction No. 6 and that the communications systems of the American and the British--air support control centers and liaison parties for lower-echelon units--were quite similar. Eisenhower's planners paid particular attention to the sensitive problem of response time, suggesting that most lost time was caused by the ground commanders who could not make up their minds. They recommended that identified targets should be forwarded ahead of time to the command center so that missions could be organized. When this was not possible, they would allow "a suitable portion of supporting combat aviation . . . be maintained on 'alert' status, either 'ground' or 'air.'" Their directive did not define a "suitable portion" of aircraft for alert status. Airmen seemed unaware of the potential for abuse of limited air resources. In any regard, the wishes of the ground commander dominated this portion of the directive.[4]

Allied planners now placed much responsibility for the air-ground system on the ground commander: "Effective air support of ground troops is dependent on a proper estimate of the situation by the supported commander." But they still

---

*Direct air support was the British term for close air support. Its use here illustrates the British influence on Allied thought processes and publications.

waffled on the level of command authority over air support. Although all air forces would "operate under the command of the Commander-in-Chief, Allied Forces," the Allied commander could allot forces to a task force commander. The task force commander would normally retain control, but he could also "designate part of his combat aviation to assist directly a specified unit of the Task Force." A clear potential existed for air support units being controlled by brigade or division commanders as well as corps or army commanders. The remarkable aspect of this Allied directive was that it ran against the trend of equality between air and ground forces being established by a successful Allied force operating in the Western Desert.[5]

The planners also included in their memorandum some long-running concerns of airmen: "As a general rule, only those targets which cannot be reached quickly and effectively by artillery should be assigned to combat aviation." Command was generally centralized, either under the commander-in-chief, Allied Forces, or under a task force commander. Probable targets would be discovered and reported by observation aircraft that, lacking radios, would report on their return to base. Most air support operations would then be planned ahead of time and often by the highest command authority rather than the battalion, regiment, or division in the field. The final line of the directive, before Brig. Gen. Walter Bedell Smith's signature block, warned about the vulnerability and scarcity of air forces: "Available direct support aviation must neither be dispersed nor frittered away on unimportant targets. The mass of such support should be reserved for concentration and overwhelming attack upon important objectives."[6]

Because most of the force for TORCH would be American, it was appropriate that British Prime Minister Winston Churchill and Roosevelt picked Eisenhower for the post of commander-in-chief, directing a small AFHQ staff. Eisenhower's task force was organized largely by national components. The desired integration of this force had to be carried out by Eisenhower's personal effort rather than through a combined organization. Ground forces were originally organized into American and British task forces, supported by the Allied Naval Expeditionary Force and the American Twelfth Air Force and British Eastern Air Command.[7]

To gather enough resources for the Twelfth Air Force, Arnold stripped the England-based Eighth Air Force of fighter, light bomber, and even some heavy bomber squadrons. These and additional units fresh from training in the United

States, and with most personnel only partially trained, were formed into three functional Twelfth Air Force components: XII Bomber Command, XII Fighter Command, and XII Air Support Command. On 23 October Maj. Gen. James H. Doolittle, just back from the raid on Japan, assumed command of these units as chief of the new Twelfth Air Force and as chief airman on Eisenhower's staff.[8]

While all three components of the Twelfth Air Force would support Eisenhower's theater mission, the XII Air Support Command had a first priority to support the Fifth Army. It would provide close air support functions of close-in bombing and strafing of enemy ground forces, air defense against enemy aircraft, and observation. It would also undertake missions not connected to the immediate needs of the ground forces, such as attacking enemy air facilities, long-range reconnaissance, and bombing and strafing deep in the enemy rear. Eisenhower agreed that the Twelfth Air Force should employ "both tactical and strategic elements" in common with the British air forces practices. By "strategic elements" he meant bombing units that could destroy distant military targets, such as air bases, shipping, ports, and communications centers.* The XII Fighter and XII Bomber Commands, indeed all Allied air resources, would be available to support TORCH ground forces as determined by the commander-in-chief. Eisenhower came to his command with a long-time interest in aviation support for the ground forces. While he wanted support for the ground forces, he also supported the strategic bombing campaign, directed by Maj. Gen. Carl Spaatz in England, because it would soften up Germany and thus facilitate success in future battles. Given his responsibilities for theater and large strategic concerns, Eisenhower was inclined to see the unity-of-command concept from the theater point of view. Consistent with Army doctrine, the theater commander controlled all resources. In turn, Eisenhower had a tendency to think of aviation, if not close air support specifically, in terms of theater rather than of army, corps, or division interests. He was more inclined, therefore, to allow the Army Air Forces to centralize air resources and have command at a higher level.[9]

Anticipating the needs of future war, Arnold and other staff airmen in Washington had developed similar concepts for command on a modern battlefield.

---

*Today "strategic elements" would be regarded as deep battlefield interdiction.

They had accepted the necessity for command decisions being made at a theater or task force level of command, but they gave this unity-of-command concept another twist when talking about joint air-ground operations. Arnold advocated the "principle of command," where the air commander would have "direct command of the tactical operations" of the air forces in air operations. During July 1942 he articulated the concept of "direct command" in a memo to Maj. Gen. Thomas T. Handy, the assistant chief of staff for operations. Arnold argued that the air commander was the specialist and that he should have control over his particular operations. He cited Maj. Gen. M. F. Harmon: "The Air Force Commanders are especially trained to appreciate the peculiar powers and limitations of the Air Arm, and are therefore particularly suited to exercise tactical command in order to realize the maximum performance of the units involved." It is not clear how much of Arnold's concept meshed with the idea of a task force concept of Eisenhower, but Eisenhower came to accept great independence among his commanders. He saw his air, ground, and naval chiefs having a dual role. First, everyone worked with Eisenhower's staff in the development of plans; then each became the responsible commander for executing his part of the whole operation.[10]

As the vagaries of war would have it, the Combined Chiefs of Staff did not establish a clear directive for Eisenhower until the last few weeks before the invasion was to take place. Eisenhower would make a three-pronged invasion of North Africa. That meant the American ground forces and supporting air forces would have to be split into three elements: one for an invasion at Oran, Algeria; another to land in French Morocco; and another, a combined British-American force under British Lt. Gen. K. A. N. Anderson, to invade at Algiers (Map 2). The role of the air forces in support of the ground forces was confused when the functional organization of an air force (into bombardment, fighter, and air support commands) was altered, with the air commands split up in their assignment to different ground invasion commands. Time was incredibly brief for gathering sufficient air support forces and for organizing them in an effective manner.

TORCH planners gave the task force commanders clear operational control of their supporting air resources. Maj. Gen. George S. Patton, Jr., sailing directly from the United States, would command the Western Task Force landing in French

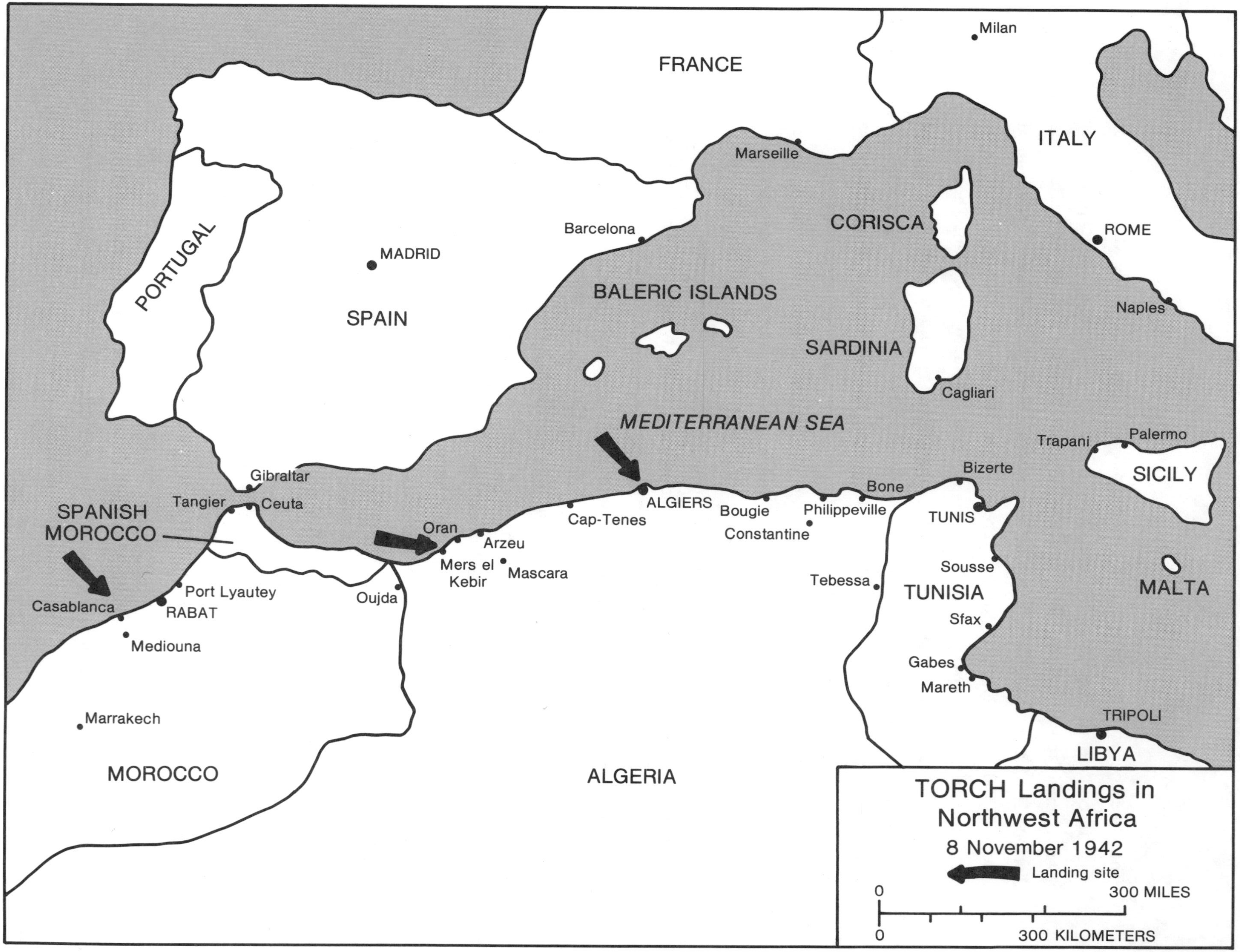
TORCH Landings in Northwest Africa
8 November 1942
Landing site
0
300 MILES
0
300 KILOMETERS
FRANCE
Milan
ITALY
ROME
Naples
Marseille
CORISCA
Barcelona
MADRID
SPAIN
PORTUGAL
BALERIC ISLANDS
SARDINIA
Cagliari
MEDITERRANEAN SEA
Trapani
Palermo
SICILY
MALTA
Bizerte
Bone
TUNIS
Sousse
TUNISIA
Sfax
Gabes
Mareth
TRIPOLI
LIBYA
Gibraltar
Tangier
Ceuta
SPANISH
MOROCCO
Casablanca
Port Lyautey
RABAT
Mediouna
Marrakech
MOROCCO
Oujda
Oran
Mers el
Kebir
Arzeu
Mascara
Cap-Tenes
ALGIERS
Bougie
Constantine
Philippeville
Tebessa
ALGERIA
MAP 2

Morocco. His command included Brig. Gen. John K. Cannon's XII Air Support Command, which also had been recently formed in the United States. Maj. Gen. Lloyd Fredendall would command the Central Task Force landing in Oran. He controlled portions of the XII Fighter and XII Bomber Commands led by Col. Lauris Norstad, Doolittle's operations officer. The multiple air services for ground support, as exemplified in an air support command, were missing in the latter case, an indication of indifference or fuzzy thinking about the kind of aircraft to be used in close air support work in North Africa.[11]

Even with the last-minute changes, TORCH planners insisted on following the dictates of British-United States air doctrine. For example, after the Oran and Casablanca ground forces won their battles and reconsolidated into the Fifth Army, the XII Air Support Command would continue to provide the single point of air support service. In addition, the bomber and fighter commands would be on call for close air support and other ground tasks; but, when not on alert, they would turn to the "normal" (planned interdiction) Air Force objectives. In a report to Patton, Doolittle agreed that ground warfare was the main focus of the theater operations. He also wanted it clarified that first priority went to air superiority and that supporting ground action came second.[12]

As envisioned by Eisenhower's planners, the Twelfth Air Force would provide communications equipment and personnel necessary to the command and control* of air units. Twelfth Air Force air support parties attached to infantry divisions and armored columns would relay air support requests to an air support control center, set up next to the task force command post. After the task force commander approved requests for air support from the subordinate units, they would be transmitted to the Twelfth Air Force. Air Force expertise would play its part at the Twelfth Air Force or the XII Air Support Command. The XII Air Support Command would then allocate missions to the appropriate subordinate fighter, bomber, or observation unit.[13]

The one British and two American forces were both casually and awkwardly

---

*Neither "command and control" nor "C[2]" were terms commonly employed in World War II. Terms like "communications" or "air support control" would be the most comparable terminology.

55

integrated. Problems resulted. The command chain, from task force commanders upwards to Eisenhower and his small AFHQ staff, was clear enough. So too was the command downward, from task force commander to supporting air forces. Connections in other directions, often necessary and useful in a combined operation, were weak. For example, in terms of aviation, Air Marshal Sir William Welsh of the Eastern Air Command, supporting the British First Army, had but very oblique coordination responsibilities for the Royal Air Force Middle East, Malta forces, and British naval aviation. As another example, the two air commanders, Welsh with the Eastern Air Command, and Doolittle with the Western Air Command that supported the American task forces, were not connected. They made their plans in isolation from one another. Planning for aviation was flawed by the separate tasking and areas of responsibilities for the ground and air support forces for the invasion. An important question asked by the planners was whether the flaws would jeopardize the invasion itself or whether they would be unimportant until forces had time to reorganize once solidly ashore.[14]

Operations: TORCH Landings and the Offensive Against Tunisia

Casualties were light during the TORCH landings, 8 November 1942, at Casablanca and at Oran and Algiers. The inexperience of the forces was very evident. Even the British forces had not absorbed lessons from the successful Eighth Army operations in Libya. Fortunately, the Vichy French, having no heart for serious battle, undertook only a short-lived delaying action. The XII Air Support Command with Patton in the Western Task Force could not get Army Air Forces aircraft off the carriers that were carrying them to the invasion shore and into action until after the surrender at Casablanca. Naval aircraft picked up the responsibility, carrying out the necessary air cooperation tasks. Only air support parties and service personnel of the XII Air Support Command became involved in the action by participating in a II Corps infantry assault. The 31st Fighter Group flew to Oran to help the naval air forces support Fredendall and his ground forces in a brief battle for Oran, but the French surrendered that city on D-Day plus 2. The Royal Air Force helped, in a minor fashion, the Eastern Assault Force, led by Maj. Gen. Charles W. Ryder. A successful assault on Algiers, in order to facilitate seizure of Tunisia, was the most important object of Operation TORCH. Algiers surrendered on the evening of D-Day.[15]

As the troops were congratulating themselves, General Anderson arrived in Algiers to start the push eastward. The British First Army and, for close air support, the Royal Air Forces' No. 242 Group, Eastern Air Command, made up the main force. Attached to Anderson's task force were a few Free French and American elements. The largest American unit was a tank regiment of Combat Command B, commanded by Col. Paul M. Robinett. Supporting American air elements, including the 60th Troop Carrier Group (C-47s), 14th Fighter Group (P-38s), and 15th Bombardment Squadron (A-20s), were employed by the Eastern Air Command within a few weeks. Six hundred miles to the east, in Tunisia, the Germans were assembling a large counterforce. Time became important, with winter rains expected in December and Rommel in full retreat before Montgomery, westward toward Tunisia.[16]

As with the TORCH landings, the Allies underestimated the opposition and problems associated with a winter campaign hundreds of miles across Algeria and Tunisia. Their planners had assumed that the Vichy French and local Arabs would not effectively deter the rush eastward and that the Axis would not build a strong defense. Air and ground leaders did not make a great effort to absorb the lessons of mobile warfare, including the revival of the principle of mass dictated by Montgomery's Eighth Army experience. Anderson led the forces with the British First Army, which was composed of one incomplete division and a few smaller units, including a small portion of the American 1st Armored Division. British tactical air forces and portions of the Twelfth Air Force provided close air support. Troops were well trained, but the force included neither experienced, battle-tested, leaders nor individual units. Anderson spread his attacking force in a north-to-south formation in the drive eastward towards Tunisia. His intent was to prevent Axis units from harassing the main drive along the coast, but the spread formation precluded concentration of forces to push through Axis defenses just then building up in Tunisia (Map 3). Allied intelligence initially underestimated Axis strength in numbers of aircraft, vehicles, and defensive weapons. Then, by the end of November, as additional Allied units were called in to beef up the attack against determined Axis air and ground forces, the logistical support broke down, and the forces at the front could not be adequately supplied.

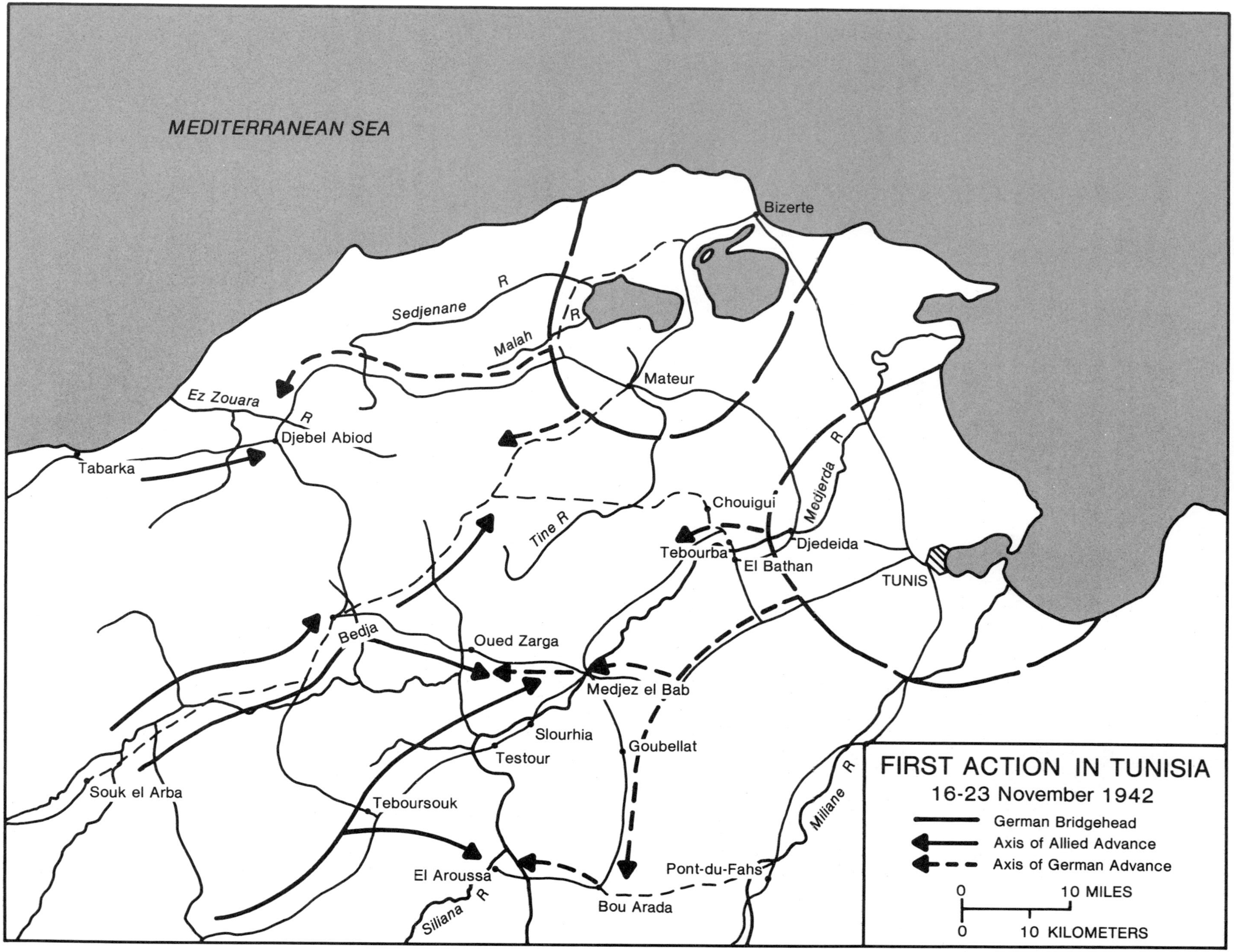
MEDITERRANEAN SEA
Bizerte
Sedjenane R
Malah R
Mateur
Ez Zouara R
Djebel Abiod
Tabarka
Chouigui
Medjerda R
Tine R
Djedeida
Tebourba
El Bathan
TUNIS
Bedja
Oued Zarga
Medjez el Bab
Slourhia
Goubellat
Testour
Souk el Arba
Teboursouk
Milliane R
Pont-du-Fahs
El Aroussa
Siliana R
Bou Arada
FIRST ACTION IN TUNISIA
16-23 November 1942
German Bridgehead
Axis of Allied Advance
Axis of German Advance
0 10 MILES
0 10 KILOMETERS
MAP 3

A host of problems affecting general operations likewise limited the air-ground support system. Long distances and inadequate transportation facilities limited logistics support for the air forces as well as the army. A lack of all-weather airfields forced units to crowd onto workable fields, and the long distances to targets limited the time Allied support aircraft could loiter over the battlefield waiting for calls from the ground (Map 4). Lack of radar and inadequate communications systems encouraged Anderson to look for alternatives in his air support. He ignored standard doctrine, for example, when he resorted to extensive employment of aircraft in defensive cover missions to try to stop the aggressive German air attacks. This left insufficient aircraft for other close air support tasks and other tactical functions, such as air superiority, supply interdiction, and reconnaissance.

In mid-November, when Anderson moved his headquarters eastward towards the Algerian-Tunisian border, he asked the Royal Air Force to carefully coordinate with his ground forces the obviously inadequate number of aircraft. Air Commodore G. M. Lawson moved into a command post next door to facilitate air-ground support. Evidence suggests that the interrelationship was not effective; Lawson was not able to control the few American units transferred to the British-led task force, raising the charge that air and ground leaders were conducting separate warfare. For their part, airmen claimed that many mission requests produced ineffective results and that aircraft were wasted on missions to satisfy demands of subordinate ground commanders. The record shows extensive air activity during the third week of November, when fighters flew nearly fifteen hundred reconnaissance and top-cover defense sorties. Unfortunately, it is never clear how many of these were conducted as close air support missions, as opposed to general air support work. Eisenhower was becoming convinced that one way to attack the problem of air support was to bring air units under the more centralized control of an air commander.

During the last week in November, when Anderson attacked with his force's greatest energy, the air arms flew nineteen hundred sorties, twice the number of the Axis. Close air support in terms of defensive covers continued, but most air missions were given to bombing the supply line and hitting shipping and air bases. The intensive air action produced heavy aircraft losses and damage that could not

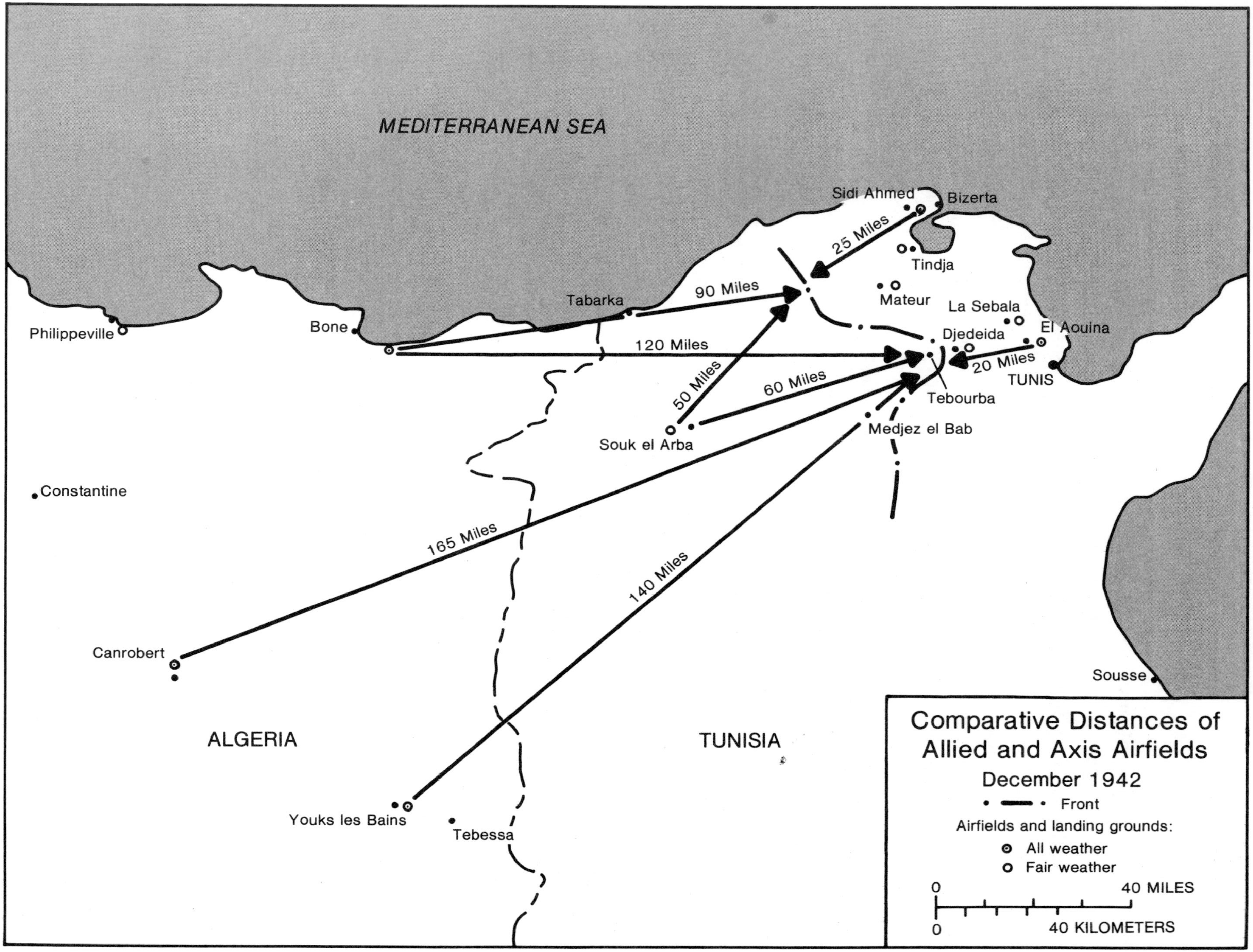
MEDITERRANEAN SEA
Sidi Ahmed
Bizerta
25 Miles
Tindja
Mateur
La Sebala
El Aouina
Djedeida
20 Miles
TUNIS
Tebourba
Medjez el Bab
Tabarka
90 Miles
Bone
Philippeville
120 Miles
50 Miles
60 Miles
Souk el Arba
Constantine
165 Miles
140 Miles
Canrobert
Sousse
ALGERIA
TUNISIA
Youks les Bains
Tebessa
Comparative Distances of
Allied and Axis Airfields
December 1942
Front
Airfields and landing grounds:
All weather
Fair weather
0
40 MILES
0
40 KILOMETERS

MAP 4

be overcome by shorthanded maintenance crews or replacement aircraft and crews. The greatest problem, according to the ground commanders, was the repeated attack by the supposedly obsolete German Stukas. Fighters would be called up for defensive cover, but because of the great distances, the fighter loitering time was brief. While the Allied aircraft were in the air, German dive bombers merely returned to their airfields and waited for the all-clear signal. Allied air forces could not provide enough continuity in their air cover.[17]

Because Allied air support forces could not stem the enemy air attacks over the battlefield, some ground commanders complained. Robinett, now a brigadier general, insisted "that men cannot stand the mental and physical strain of constant aerial bombing without feeling that all possible is being done to beat enemy air efforts." Brig. Gen. Terry Allen, commander of the U.S. 1st Infantry Division during the invasion of Oran, suggested that division command staffs should include an air adviser. Allen had been assigned a temporary air adviser, Col. Harold Fowler, during the landing assault, to help plan air support for the ground forces. Allen saw great weakness in the "on call" air support by which requests went up through the various levels of army command and down through the air force echelons. The method was too slow. He wanted a system that assured "prompt air support against anticipated targets in the zone of advance of the major effort."[18]

Eisenhower agreed that enemy "strafing and dive-bombing" were responsible for stopping the attempted advances of the First Army. Anderson suggested that unless the enemy attacks could be reduced, Allied forces would have to withdraw to a position where they could get cover. The ground commanders were even more adamant about cover because they did not see or know of reciprocal air attacks against enemy troops. Eisenhower and Anderson were probably unaware that Churchill, in reference to use of the air umbrella in the Western Desert the year previous, had forbidden the use of aircraft in troop-cover operations because it was a waste of resources. The air doctrine of both Allied forces also rejected employment of air cover as an inefficient use of air resources. Nevertheless, the orders of insistent ground commanders carried weight, and airmen continued assigning ineffective air cover missions. When the battle got worse for the Allies, airmen pointed to improper employment of air cover as an important cause for failure. But the air forces failed in other areas of air support. Fighter groups continued their offensive air missions against enemy air bases and air defense over friendly forces, but were not trained for strafing. Light bombers, originally designed for close air support work, proved useless against well-protected targets and were assigned night bombardment duties, which minimized enemy defensive fire from aircraft or ground antiaircraft artillery. The Allies had no effective ground attack aircraft until mid-December, when they brought in some modified P-40s and Hurricanes that would serve as fighter-bombers.[19]

Believing that victory in Tunisia depended on full employment of air power, and the fact that the ground forces were unable to break Axis defense, Eisenhower halted the offensive. Winter rains and mud made the operations difficult throughout December. Ground forces, with supporting air units, probed at weaknesses in the German lines, but the offense was uncoordinated and opportunistic. Until mid-January, Allied operations aimed at local consolidation and keeping pressure on the enemy. The air forces started work on new airfields closer to the battlefield. Eastern Air Command and Twelfth Air Force bombers continued the interdiction attacks on ports, supply dumps, shipping, and airfields in Tunisia and Sicily, but generally the enemy retained air superiority in the region.[20]

Operations: Reorganization and the Second Tunisian Offensive

While many Twelfth Air Force units had been released to aid the First Army in November and December of 1942, Allied leaders held back a number of units in western Algeria and Morocco, and assigned them to protect the lines of communications with Gibraltar and England. The usefulness of these units for operations against the Axis was limited, because personnel and units lacked operational training and because poor transportation facilities prevented supply and maintenance of additional troops on the battlefront. In view of his dual mission to protect the lines of communications in Morocco and Algeria and to support Anderson's drive against Tunisia in November, Doolittle began organizing the air forces into flexible composite commands, each with a specific geographic area of responsibility.

By the end of December Eisenhower, more satisfied with the pacification of Morocco and Algeria and willing to increase force strength for the campaign in

Tunisia, invalidated the need for Doolittle's small composite air forces. Rather, Eisenhower agreed with ground and air commanders that the time was ripe for a centralized air command in the Mediterranean, to coordinate the air forces better. On 5 January 1943, with British concurrence, he instituted a new layer in the air command structure, designating a new air force headquarters, the Allied Air Forces, at his headquarters in Algiers. He appointed his air adviser, General Spaatz, commander of this Allied Air Force. Spaatz had great influence organizing the British and American air effort in Tunisia, but he had difficulty coordinating the widely separated air units because communications was crude and inadequately supplied. AFHQ, the headquarters of British and American armies, the Navy, and even the Allied Air Force were in different locations in Algeria and Morocco. Sometimes motorcycles were the only available means for transmitting messages and command instructions.

Eisenhower also accepted the British concept of dividing major mission responsibilities by function rather than by national consideration. Nevertheless, a tendency of maintaining national unity in lower echelons prevailed throughout the war. The reorganization again left close air support functions without central direction on the battlefield. In the new Allied air force structure Doolittle's bomber organization would specialize in deep-strike bombing missions, and the Royal Air Force would specialize in air-ground support. Eisenhower assigned Air Commodore Lawson the task of close air support for British First Army. When American forces began to be deployed, Eisenhower could not resist letting the American airmen support American ground forces, and the Twelfth Air Force carried out support to the American ground forces in Tunisia, as well as its bombing missions.[21]

In January 1943 Eisenhower decided to intensify efforts in central Tunisia; favorable weather conditions promised better results along the coast, where mud and strong defensive positions slowed Anderson's First Army (Map 5). Eisenhower designated Fredendall's II Corps as the principal ground force for the advance against the German communications line that ran north to south through Tunisia. Important to later events, a new Free French element was slipped in between the American and British forces operating in the north. Remaining at Algiers, Eisenhower assumed direct command of military operations on the entire front,

American Battlefield in Southern Tunsia

exercising that command through a ground deputy, Brig. Gen. Lucian K. Truscott, Jr., stationed at Constantine, a hundred or so miles from the front. Spaatz, as Eisenhower's staff air officer, and the Twelfth Air Force played an integral part in AFHQ planning. Spaatz directed air force operations of continuing interest to the theater, including close air support; interdiction against Axis forces, shipping, ports, and airfields; reconnaissance service; and air defense. Spaatz also surveyed the battlefield with Maj. Gen. Mark W. Clark in an attempt to develop better cooperation between air and ground units.[22]

Eisenhower moved the XII Air Support Command from Morocco and, following previous procedures, attached it to II Corps. Spaatz sought to tie the air and ground forces together by appointing a XII Air Support colonel to serve as liaison officer with the British First Army and by dedicating airplanes to both of the major ground commanders, Anderson and Fredendall. Brig. Gen. Howard A. Craig, who replaced Cannon as the commander of the XII Air Support Command, outlined a conventional air support plan: He would locate his headquarters next to II Corps Headquarters; his fighter and light bomber groups would serve as the basic force, but other Twelfth Air Force units could be called in as necessary; an advanced operations command post would help control air units in the advanced combat area; and air support parties with HF and VHF radio sets would be attached to combat commands or teams.[23]

Craig's plans indicated that close air support missions would be a large part of the XII Air Support Command's efforts but that other tactical missions were important as well, and ground commanders would have to appreciate certain air limitations. He stipulated that air missions be planned in advance and that extemporaneous calls for air support be kept to a minimum. Prior to D-Day, all available air units would reconnoiter the front and flanks of the advance route. Fighter sweeps would hit enemy air installations and, joining with light bombers, they would attack any enemy counteroffense. Close air support air cover for the advancing forces would be "provided only at critical places and for limited periods." For full daylight cover, other Twelfth Air Force fighter aircraft would have to be called into the campaign. Orders for missions would come from the Air Support Command. Craig asserted that the Air Support Command would exert a maximum effort against previously identified enemy targets, but that a large portion of the air strength would be held "in readiness for calls from the Air Support Parties with the several elements of the Division and Corps."[24]

On 17 January II Corps was just beginning a forward movement in central Tunisia when it was preempted by a German counterattack at a weak spot in the line--the French defenders located between the Americans in the south and British forces in northern Tunisia. The British 6th Armoured Division as well as Robinett's armor moved to the aid of the retreating French. The action was over quickly. By the twenty-fifth the German advance was halted. The Royal Air Force's tactical air organization, No. 242 Group, put up daily fighter-bomber sorties, but the XII Air Support Command gave only minor aid during the eight days of defensive action. Post-battle evaluation suggested several reasons for lack of aid from the XII Air Support Command, including an inhibiting enemy air superiority, inadequate command and control of available close air resources, and ineffective tactics.[25] In an interview Maj. Gen. Lunsford E. Oliver, who had been Combat Command B commander earlier, suggested that, with enemy air superiority, ground forces needed a quicker response time when they requested air support. The system of requests going up and down command echelons was too slow. Instead, "We've got to be able to call for our support planes that are actually in the air."[26]

The first intense encounters with German forces revealed a flaw in American support bombardment tactics. Their use of light and medium bombers for low-level close air support missions proved disastrous because of effective German light antiaircraft artillery. Arnold's fears about the new bombers were justified. The A-20, B-25, and B-26 crews were forced to high altitude operations while in the middle of combat operations. While flying at a new altitude of 10,000 feet was not difficult, trying to hit targets using crude bomb sights and flying in formation proved impossible without intense training. The airmen had some succcess experimenting with the British fighter-bomber technique using bomb-carrying fighters to attack front-line targets. Fighter resources were overstrained, however, trying to provide escort for bombers and area defense for airfields and for the ground operations attacked by offensive-minded Axis air forces.

There was blame for all. Although poor training and inadequate numbers of aircraft were at the heart of the complaints from the II Corps, airmen also found fault with II Corps' ignorance of Army air doctrine. For example, the II Corps commander, Fredendall, refused a request for air reconnaissance from the French, suggesting that the French sector was not his responsibility. In another instance Spaatz felt it was necessary to come to Fredendall's headquarters to complain about the improper use of reconnaissance aircraft. Contrary to Spaatz's orders, Fredendall had ordered light bomber missions over enemy territory, when the bombers were equipped with sensitive gear that would jeopardize Allied security if captured. Spaatz insisted that Fredendall should not attempt to operate the air resources without a knowledgeable airman by his side and that the XII Air Support Command commander, Craig, should control the air resources until air and ground headquarters could be joined. Eisenhower recognized the difficulty of coordinating forces across national lines, and taking a cue from Allied leaders at Casablanca, on 21 January he assigned Anderson coordinating responsibilities for all Allied forces.[27]

At the same time, Eisenhower ordered his staff air operations officer, Brig. Gen. Laurence S. Kuter, to command all Allied air support operations. Within a few days, Eisenhower recognized the difficulty for Anderson to coordinate independent commands spread over a broad front. On 26 January Anderson was given command over the Allied forces in the Tunisian offensive. Kuter was now directly responsible to Anderson, and he located his headquarters with Anderson's at Constantine. Kuter's Allied Air Support Command coordinated missions for the XII Air Support Command and the No. 242 Group and passed bombing requests to Twelfth Air Force and Eastern Air Command. Always concerned with theater strategy, Eisenhower informed Anderson that the Allied air forces would continue to attack Rommel's communications lines. The command arrangement developed by Eisenhower began to resemble even more the air forces doctrinal model for centralized theater control of air.[28]

On 30 January the Germans launched their second of three major offensives against the Allies in Tunisia, this one also against the French sector. Eisenhower attached II Corps under the command of the British First Army, although Anderson in turn directed Fredendall to command all ground forces in the area of attack. Anderson and Fredendall did not have a system to coordinate the air support, except through the efforts of Kuter at Allied Air Support Command. Close air support promised to be a problem, and the likelihood of a problem was increased by the appointment of a new commander for the XII Air Support Command. Col. Paul L. Williams had a reputation of being compliant to ground commanders. He also carried less rank and influence than Craig.

For five days Allied forces fought a defensive battle, finally retreating to stronger positions. Again, Allied air could not gain superiority over Axis air and was still too weak to play a decisive role against the Axis ground advance. With assistance from Rommel's German Desert Air Force and the Italian air forces, which had been forced back by the British in the east, the Axis kept effective control of the air over Tunisia. In the middle of the battle German Stukas laid a vicious attack on the 1st Armored Division's Combat Command D.* Ground commanders again asked for more air cover. Williams directed some strafing and bombing attacks against German assault forces in direct support of Allied ground operations. He allocated aircraft for interdiction strikes, especially at communications in the German rear. He also coordinated with Kuter's Allied Air Support Command the employment of other air organizations, including some interdiction missions by the Twelfth Air Force fighters and bombers, even the B-17s normally used for more distant targets, against the German rear.

Williams also complied with the ground commander's requests for a defensive air umbrella, and on one occasion, on 1 February, his fighter cap caught and broke up attacking Stuka and Messerschmitt Me-109 fighter escort formations. However, the intense activity in close air support and other tactical missions extracted a price from XII Air Support Command resources. Flying organizations were debilitated. For example, the most experienced fighter unit, the 33d Fighter Group, suffered so many losses it was forced into retirement in Morocco for regrouping. Air and ground leaders learned about the attrition of air resources in air-ground missions, namely, that aircraft were easily used up and as vulnerable as air doctrine suggested. Leaders also recognized that defensive air operations, especially covers flown on a broad-fronted war, used up all available resources. Either more aircraft were needed to respond to the requests of the ground commanders or Williams would have to allocate his aircraft more judiciously.[29]

---

*The 1st Armored Division was organized into four subunits to facilitate separate taskings: Combat Commands A, B, C, and D.

Eisenhower felt that the Army's failure stemmed from the confusion of battle and inexperience of the troops, who were unable to maintain their composure in combat. He told Fredendall, Anderson, Spaatz, and other subordinate commanders that battle losses were caused "by failure of officers to carry out orders, by men failing to construct foxholes or slit trenches, by disregard of orders requiring use of vehicle blackout lights, by running vehicle columns closed up." He believed the troops had insufficient antiaircraft defenses, and he suggested that additional training was needed to teach ground troops not only that enemy dive bombers were vulnerable to small arms fire but also that they should "fire with every available weapon against enemy aircraft within range."[30] Eisenhower turned to the experienced Mideast British commanders for guidance.

Eisenhower did not criticize the published air-ground doctrine; rather, he indicated that the problem with close air support operations lay in the need for air and ground forces to "get together in training. . . ."[31] He called for the inculcation of existing doctrine. At the air support command level Williams also approved the basic doctrine in FM 31-35. Both men suggested that the combat practices were distorting some of the doctrine, especially the defensive stance necessary for air cover. Airmen had consistently asserted, and published doctrine stated, that air umbrellas overtaxed the limited resources and were, by their very nature, incomplete and ineffective. In addition, if the air support commander allocated his resources for a widespread defensive cover, he would be unable to concentrate his forces for the air superiority campaign. The only way to stop the enemy air attack, according to current Army Air Force doctrine, was to give it the highest priority and destroy aircraft in offensive air actions and attacks on enemy air bases. At Eisenhower's headquarters Kuter asserted that the German dive bomber attack on Combat Command D marked the only time American troops suffered greatly under destructive German air attack, even though Stukas attacked on several occasions. In summary, air and ground leaders at theater level agreed that the air and ground forces put great effort into close air support but failed to apply published doctrine. It would take more education and training to change the ground commanders' minds on the danger of Stukas before they would decrease their demands for increased air support. Close air support practices and doctrine were not yet in accord on the battlefield.[32]

Operations: Kasserine and a New Look at Close Air Support

In mid-February 1943 the Axis attacked in central Tunisia again.[33] This time Rommel, who had been retreating westward across Tripolitania, running from Montgomery and the British Eighth Army, gathered enough forces to hit the center of the Allied line in Tunisia. The forewarned II Corps forces were just then preparing a defense. Rommel attempted to split Eisenhower's Allied forces in Western Tunisia while protecting his flank from Montgomery's forces. Counterattacking, French and British forces, as well as II Corps units in the region, took heavy losses, even though commanders concentrated the bulk of the Allied air support resources and ground forces in the central region. Troops could not protect airfields and artillery brigades, which were overrun. Tanks, half-tracks, and mobile artillery were captured and destroyed by the hundreds. Strengthened with British armor, Fredendall tried to maintain a defense in Kasserine Pass on 18 February, but German units overcame Allied defenders and poured through the pass on the nineteenth.

The XII Air Support Command ordered missions, but the effort was diminished because the forward bases were lost and aircraft were forced to fly greater distances for fuel and munitions. The Allied Air Support Command in Constantine reinforced the defense by calling in additional Twelfth Air Force resources, including medium and heavy bombers, fighters, and transports. Light bomber and fighter units tried to furnish defensive cover over retreating Allied troops. Success was mixed with failure. On one occasion fighter-bombers had appreciable effect bombing and strafing enemy infantry, guns, and tanks. On another occasion friendly ground fire was deadly to the air forces--on 21 and 22 February, Combat Command B antiaircraft fire turned back American flights, destroying five planes and damaging other friendly ground attack aircraft.

On the twenty-second British Tommies and Churchill tanks stopped a German Panzer unit near the border of Tunisia and Algeria, an event which seemed to take the spirit out of Rommel's offensive. On the twenty-third, with great effort, the Allies counterattacked and pushed the Germans back through the pass. Hoping to conserve his tanks for the continuing fight against the British Eighth Army, Rommel pulled his forces into defensive positions in the next range of mountains to the east. The battle around the Kasserine turned out to be the last serious Axis offensive effort in Africa.

The Allied debacle at Kasserine exposed some structural as well as technological failings and underestimations about necessary force strength to battle the Axis powers. Allied forces in Tunisia were not as experienced in mobile warfare as the Axis or Allied forces in the Western Desert. Both air and ground force leaders assessed air support as ineffective. As usual, the ground forces commanders got less air support than they wanted. Some crippling problems, common to battle, limited the effectiveness of air operations. Like many ground units, air squadrons had been overrun by Rommel's attack. Forward bases, fuel, bombs, and supplies had to be abandoned or destroyed. Disrupted communications caused by the retreating defense hampered interaction. A more dramatic limitation resulted from bad flying weather from 18 to 21 February. Even heavy bombers, called in for the occasion, could not find targets through the overcast. Not until the twenty-second, during the repulse, could the Allied air forces help significantly. The Allies were not alone in blaming the weather for their performances. Rommel attested to the bad weather. He blamed his failed offense on weather that grounded the Luftwaffe.

Complaints and commentary about air support came from every direction. The attack by enemy aircraft was intense enough to cause many ground troops to shoot at any plane in sight. Pilots complained about fire from friendly forces, and the situation was desperate enough to cause Combat Command B Commander Robinett to order that his troops not fire on any aircraft until after an attacker showed national colors. Doolittle suggested, unsuccessfully, that the Allies should stop ground operations and undertake an intensive air campaign to destroy the enemy air forces before continuing the Tunisian campaign. Even Churchill complained about the air support operations, blasting the failure of the Allied forces to build up satisfactory air superiority when so many first-line aircraft and large numbers of support personnel had been committed to aviation in Tunisia. The prime minister also suggested that the apparent inadequacy of allocated resources pointed to the need for an even greater allotment of war materials for Tunisia. Americans had been expected to provide the quantity necessary to win the war, and military leaders could be rightfully embarrassed when these battles in Tunisia pointed to a failure of their arms. The airmen began to realize that a tough enemy required even more resources than originally conceived and that greater intensity and commitment were needed to defeat the Axis.

Of all the critics, none was more influential than British Air Vice Marshal Sir Arthur Coningham, who replaced Kuter as commander of the centralized Allied Air Support Command during the Kasserine operation. While Eisenhower was opposed to the British "committee system"* of command, he also advocated a commander having the flexibility to organize forces to suit national proclivities, and he gave Coningham the freedom to operate by his own style. Coningham now helped convince Eisenhower and other high-level Allied leaders that close air support forces must be organized on a basis of scarcity and that, in particular, ground commanders could not expect as much close air support as they heretofore thought necessary. In the context of military reversals, such as Kasserine, the senior leaders of the Tunisian campaign found the economy-of-force principle more acceptable.

Coningham ultimately discontinued several other Tunisian cooperative practices, some first seen when he took over the Western Desert Air Force. He criticized the defensive air cover flying mode, then used by the XII Air Support Command and No. 242 Group. With the scarcity concept accepted, he promoted the centralization of all tactical air resources under his control as air specialist on the staff of the highest field commander. Division and corps commanders would have to request close air support through the highest army commander. Although they were primarily associated with their national force, the XII Air Support Command and No. 242 Group would be commanded by Coningham rather than by the II Corps or British First Army commanders. Coningham condemned the former employment practice of having fighters on call and assigning them piecemeal to a variety of targets that were not critical to the battle. He proclaimed that, henceforth, air support missions would be offensive, with fighters seeking out the enemy's air force at or near Axis bases. For ground attack missions, enemy

---

*The British met in committee and argued collectively for consensus on a decision, whereas the American military system placed decision-making authority in the hands of a single commander.

concentrations and soft-skinned vehicles, rather than tanks, would be appropriate targets. Centralized control was a fundamental premise of Coningham's air support concept. In view of limited air resources, all aircraft units should be used in the highest priority missions. None could be held in reserve for the future use of a currently inactive ground unit. Coningham, or another air commander fully conversant with air capabilities, would determine allocation and employment upon the ground commander's determination of objectives.

Coningham's opinions were important because the Combined Chiefs of Staff saw him as a natural to command all tactical air resources in the new Mediterranean Theater organization arranged at Casablanca in January 1943. He was the primary choice for tactical command because of his success in combat operations. Coningham saw a need to reform and remodel Allied forces in Tunisia, like the successful Western Desert Army and Western Desert Air Force combination that was, just then, destroying Rommel's forces in Libya. Allied leaders in Casablanca endorsed his plan of operations when they gave him control over American and British air support forces in the Mediterranean, forces which were renamed as "tactical" air forces at that time.

The Casablanca reorganization resulted partially from a need to unify or centralize command of all forces converging around Tunisia, to prepare for the next strategic offensive, and to answer some of the weaknesses apparent in the Tunisian command organization. Instead of separate commands in the western and eastern sides of North Africa, forces were centralized under Eisenhower's command. Instead of close air support commanded directly by an army, corps, or task force commander, a tactical headquarters filtered requests and requirements. Centralization of air resources, including the centralized tactical forces under Coningham, followed substantially the British model of organizing equality between air and ground commanders in field operations, with the exception of a single commander at the theater level. The Combined Chiefs of Staff appointed Eisenhower commander-in-chief of all Mediterranean forces and gave him three British deputy commanders, one each for air, ground, and sea. They appointed General Sir Harold R. L. G. Alexander as the overall ground force commander with the title of chief of the 18th Army Group. The British First and Eighth Armies were the two principal ground force subordinates of this new group. The U.S. II Corps, commanded by Fredendall, Patton, and then Maj. Gen. Omar N. Bradley, in succession, represented the smaller American contingent reporting to the 18th Army Group. Air Chief Marshal Sir Arthur Tedder became the chief of all air units, excepting naval aviation, in the Mediterranean Air Command, with its three regional air forces: Northwest African Air Forces, Malta Air Command, and Middle East Command (Chart 2).

The Northwest African Air Forces (NAAF), commanded by Spaatz, was the largest and most important air organization in the Tunisian campaign. Although Allied leaders divided NAAF into functional units--strategic, tactical, and coastal air forces; service and training commands; and a photographic reconnaissance wing--the primary purpose of NAAF was almost exclusively tactically oriented. The mission was to cooperate with the land force. Either directly or indirectly, the forces were dedicated to furthering the advance of the land campaign. Along with the indirect interdiction missions, the tactical forces had a specific charge to provide close air support. Under Coningham, the No. 242 Group worked with the British First Army; the Western Desert Air Force worked with Montgomery and the Eighth Army; and the XII Air Support Command worked with the U.S. II Corps.

The Combined Chiefs of Staff gave Coningham the title of commander of Northwest African Tactical Air Force (NATAF), the new organization providing air support to the forces in Africa. NATAF "coincided" with the Army group level controlling all air support units dedicated to the ground forces. Programmed to be implemented at the end of February, when Montgomery's forces were scheduled to enter southern Tunisia, Allied leaders precipitated an early reorganization because of the German Kasserine offensive. The mixture of American and British officers on theater and field staffs served to give the more experienced British greater influence. Certainly, in the case of air support doctrine, Coningham's methodology, learned in the Western Desert, was pressed on American air support units. Many of Coningham's ideas were not unique to British air support. For example, Eisenhower had already centralized army command under Anderson and had directed Spaatz to coordinate air support through the Allied Air Support Command formed in January.[34]

Coningham had the reputation to sway the debate on some of the fine points separating ground and air force versions of ground support doctrine. On the concept of central control, airmen were pleased. Many ground commanders in

Tunisia, including the two major British and American army field generals, Anderson and Fredendall, sought to use close air support aircraft to protect the ground troops from enemy air attacks through constant air cover; to attack targets immediately in front of the ground forces (like flying artillery); and, as observation platforms, to watch close-in and more distant troop movements. Anderson had not yet absorbed the doctrine of the Western Desert force; Fredendall had not agreed with some of the points regarding organization, selective mission assignment, and centralized command of air support, as expressed in contemporary War Department publications or in Eisenhower's directive published before the TORCH landings.

Air leaders in Tunisia had been generally disappointed with Fredendall's practices, especially when combat had shown that air cover and constant alerts could not be carried out without an extraordinarily large air support force. Indeed, Allied leaders recognized that more aircraft were needed in North Africa. Before Kasserine and before Coningham's arrival in the Tunisian sector, the argument between Spaatz and Kuter on one side and Frendendall and Anderson on the other was more of a political tussle, with compromises that pleased no one. Ideas were bent, but the distinctive air and ground perspectives remained philosophically intact.

Coningham instituted subtle but important changes that challenged the previous way of doing business and gave air leaders greater control and influence in wartime air tactics. The air marshal divided tactical units into fighter and fighter-bomber organizations--the latter for close air support. He removed the light bombers from the air support units and put them under a tactical bomber organization that was centralized at a higher level, under Coningham at NATAF. Planning for air operations would be "determined by the air commander within the framework of the Army-Air plan approved by the Army commander." The air plan was as important as the ground plan: "The conception of making an army plan and then asking what air assistance can be provided for it will result in air power being overlooked during the important preliminary phases. . . ."[35]

Coningham boldly promoted the idea of independent air support with an endorsement from the successful Eighth Army commander, Montgomery. The British commander wanted other ground commanders to appreciate some basic aspects of air warfare. Coningham distributed to all air and ground commanders a

Montgomery-inspired pamphlet that was aimed directly at the subject of control of close air support by ground generals. The pamphlet, illustrating many aspects of a complex air warfare, proclaimed successful British principles:

> Any officer who aspires to hold high command in war must understand clearly certain basic principles regarding the use of air power.
>
> The greatest asset of air power is its flexibility . . . the flexibility inherent in Air Forces permits them . . . to be switched quickly from one objective to another in the theatre of operations. So long as this is realized, then the whole weight of the available air power can be used in selected areas in turn. This concentrated use of the air striking force is a battle-winning factor of the first importance.
>
> It follows that control of the available air power must be centralized and command must be exercised through Air Force channels. Nothing could be more fatal to successful results than to dissipate the air resources into small packets placed under command of army formation commanders, with each packet working on its own plan. The soldier must not expect or wish, to exercise direct command over air striking forces.
>
> Two adjacent HQs will provide the associated military and air commanders with the best opportunity of working together successfully. Physical proximity by itself will not produce the answer, unless it carries with it close individual contacts, a constant exchange of information and a frank interchange of views.[36]

On 16 February, in a presentation to Eisenhower and other Allied senior officers, Coningham briefed the leaders on the major ideas of duality in modern combat concepts, where air and ground leaders must recognize the difference, the coequality, and the need to cooperate as one united entity, as was evident in the Montgomery-Coningham team:

> The Soldier commands the land forces, the Airman commands the air forces; both commanders work together and operate their respective forces in accordance with a combined Army-Air plan, the whole operations being directed by the Army Commander.
>
> The Army fights on a front that may be divided into sectors, such as a Brigade, Division, Corps or an Army front. The Air front is indivisible.
>
> The Army has one battle to fight, the land battle. The Air has two. It has first of all to beat the enemy air, so that it may go into the land battle against the enemy land forces with the maximum possible hitting power.
>
> The fighter governs the front, and this fact forces the centralization of air control into the hands of one air commander operating on that front.

> You will notice that the Army Commander does not use the word "co-operation." I submit that we in Eighth Army are beyond the co-operation stage, and that work is so close that we are, in effect, one unit.[37]

While most Allied airmen found Coningham's program acceptable, Coningham knew he had a difficult task to convince Allied field generals, especially if they would see fewer friendly aircraft over the battlefield. Coningham sent propaganda material to all leaders in the theater. The success of Montgomery and failure of Allied forces in western Tunisia helped sell the point. When Eisenhower and Alexander gave their approval, the implementation followed regardless of opinions of the field commanders. Some ground commanders disagreed and continued the debate.[38]

Coningham tried to serve the needs of the ground forces. During the Allied counteroffensive against German forces in Kasserine, Coningham issued a directive to all airmen in NATAF: Maximum effort would be provided to support land operations; achieving and maintaining a high degree of air superiority would achieve that aim; and, with ground forces unhindered by enemy air attack, the air forces could give greater assistance to objectives in the rear battlefield area.[39]

As commander of NAAF and as Coningham's superior, Spaatz quietly supported the new changes for tactical aviation. He reported that ground troops were encouraged to support themselves, using antiaircraft guns against dive bomber attacks. If fighters developed an offensive against enemy air, then: "Fighter forces can be used with economy not only to protect our ground forces against dive bombing attacks . . . but also effectively to engage the enemy in the struggle for air superiority." But Spaatz was also sensitive to the occasional cross-directions of air and ground leaders. He was very busy in the next few months keeping peace between irritated air and ground leaders. He ordered that greater effort be given to develop many close air support functions, including tactical reconnaissaince and fighter-bomber and level-bombing attack techniques. He saw the great need for training and perceived the importance of personality in "the proper coordination of air effort with ground effort."[40]

Back in the United States, Arnold's staff closely watched Coningham's activities and examined his doctrinal statements. Many air and ground staff officers had studied reports about close air support in the Western Desert. Some argued against the Casablanca decision to divide forces into strategic and tactical forces because it implied the very thing they were trying to avoid, namely, division of forces into separate inflexible entities. Arnold continued to advocate continuance of the radical strategic mission, dividing the air forces into tactical and strategic combat roles to ensure that division. Kuter, fresh from the front, became the chief spokesman for the new air support concept. In mid-May, Arnold called Kuter from his assignment as deputy commander of NATAF and made him assistant air chief of staff for plans.[41]

Marshall and the War Department agreed that the North Africa campaign pointed to a revision of doctrine. Eisenhower authorized formation of a committee of air and ground officers to work with the General Staff, G-3 Division, and in short order the committee produced a newly formulated FM 100-20, Command and Employment of Air Power. Approved by Marshall and the War Department, the manual was published on 21 July 1943. The new doctrine acknowledged Coningham's emphasis on the flexibility of air power and need for centralized control under a knowledgeable air force commander, and that the theater commander would exercise command of air forces through the air force commander.

In some ways FM 100-20 was not especially innovative compared to prewar doctrinal statements in field manuals and directives, especailly the 1942 FM 31-35, Aviation in Support of Ground Forces. The contents suggested that the aviators' expertise should carry weight in employment of air resources; that the theater commander still made the final decisions on the disposition of ground and air resources, as in FM 31-35; and, paralleling Eisenhower's pre-TORCH directive, that "aviation units must not be parceled out as the advantage of massed air action and flexibility will be lost." Finally, FM 100-20 argued that close air support must be used prudently because "in the zone of contact, missions against hostile units are most difficult to control, are most expensive, and are, in general, least effective. Targets are small, well-dispersed, and difficult to locate. In addition, there is always a considerable chance of striking friendly forces. . . ."[42]

What was new about FM 100-20 was its frank proclamation of air power equality in joint warfare: "THE AIR STRIKING FORCE IS A BATTLE WINNING FACTOR OF THE FIRST IMPORTANCE." It stated explicitly that "LAND POWER

AND AIR POWER ARE CO-EQUAL AND INTERDEPENDENT FORCES; NEITHER IS AN AUXILIARY OF THE OTHER." The manual asserted that a theater commander would exercise command of ground forces through an air force commander and command of ground forces through a ground force commander. Since the greatest asset of air power was its flexibility, "CONTROL OF AVAILABLE AIR POWER MUST BE EXERCISED THROUGH THE AIR FORCE COMMANDER (caps in original). . . ."[43]

It continued to argue, in bold type, that the first priority of tactical aviation was gaining air superiority. TORCH planners had recognized the importance of air superiority, but the new manual suggested that without it victory was unlikely: "LAND FORCES OPERATING WITHOUT AIR SUPERIORITY MUST TAKE SUCH EXTENSIVE SECURITY MEASURES AGAINST HOSTILE AIR ATTACK THAT THEIR MOBILITY AND ABILITY TO DEFEAT THE ENEMY LAND FORCES ARE GREATLY REDUCED (caps in original)." The manual implied that air components must have overwhleming strength relative to opposing enemy air capabilities.[44]

More problematic to the establishment of good joint relationships and cooperative feelings, the manual established air interdiction and close air support as second and third priorities, respectively. The manual clearly implied that close air support had been subordinated, even though it emphasized positive goals of closely coordinating the air and land elements: "The destruction of selected objectives in the battle area in furtherance of the combined air-ground effort, teamwork, mutual understanding, and cooperation are essential for the success of the combined effort in the battle area." The document directed that cooperation would be carried out by "timely planning conferences of pertinent commanders and staffs, and through the exchange of liaison officers," and that air and ground liaison officers would be "well versed in air and ground tactics."[45]

Some ground force proponents in Washington and field commanders in North Africa were astounded. FM 100-20 had been approved without consulting McNair and the Army Ground Forces planners. However, the new doctrine was instituted immediately in Army ground school teachings. For example, in June 1943, a month before 100-20 was published, the Infantry School at Fort Benning, Georgia, ran a lead article on the new air-ground doctrine in its monthly journal, <u>The Mailing List</u>. (See illustrations from the journal on following pages).

The primary aim of the tactical air force is to establish and maintain air superiority. Once air superiority has been obtained, air and ground forces can carry on the battle with little interference by enemy planes. Air superiority is obtained by attacking enemy airdromes and by destroying enemy planes on the ground and in the air. The battle for the capture of German forces in Tunisia began, according to General Kuter, with the attack of German airdromes by 90 night bombers. B-26's and A-20's took up the daytime attack. By the time the ground forces pushed off three days later, 112 German planes had been destroyed.

Isolation of the battlefield is the second priority task of the tactical air force. This includes the disruption of enemy lines of communication, the destruction of supply dumps, installations and enemy troop concentrations in rear areas. If the enemy is denied food, ammunition, and reinforcements, swift, aggressive action by the ground forces will put him to rout. B-26's, shown above blasting enemy railroad lines, were used effectively for this purpose in the North African campaign.

Air missions against hostile ground units in the field of battle are the most difficult to control, the most expensive, and the least effective. For these reasons, these missions are lowest on the order of priority for missions of the tactical air force. However, their successful execution is essential to the combined air-ground effort. The P-51 shown above is strafing an enemy artillery position. In the Sicilian campaign, the A-36 fighter-bomber (the P-51 equipped with dive brakes and wing bomb racks) specialized in attacking such small but worthwhile targets as truck convoys, trains, tanks, and artillery.

In Africa Eisenhower's headquarters accepted and promoted the new air-ground relationship. In a sense, field commanders felt that they were forced to cooperate, in contradiction to Coningham's theme of a team spirit between ground and air forces. Eisenhower told Arnold that he agreed with the changes made with the air forces and that he had great faith in his chief air adviser, Spaatz, although the British charge that the "Air Force is subordinate to the Ground Forces" alarmed him. He implied that the battlefield in North Africa was bigger than doctrinal statements when he suggested that in a theater "where the character of the problem makes it predominantly air, we try to put an airman in charge; where the immediate problem is operations of Ground Forces, we make the top boss the Ground." After Kasserine, air and ground commanders, taking the new doctrinal statement with a grain of salt, immediately began to work out more practical, real-world solutions for close air support in joint operations.[46]

Close Air Support After Kasserine

As the weather improved in March 1943, air commanders expanded their activities. Additional support aircraft, airfields, and supplies diluted some complaints from the ground forces. Air planning became more an integral part of the theater campaign planning. The airmen moved in as an integral part of Alexander's 18th Army Group.[47] As Kuter described the scene: "Alexander controlled the land forces in the battle area. Coningham controlled the air forces in the battle area." The two commanders held daily consultations, making "their plans together, each stating what his force could contribute toward the general victory. They worked in complete harmony." In some cases, factors important to the air forces, such as need for close-in airfields and radar sites, were given attention.[48]

As Montgomery's forces joined the western Tunisian force, combined efforts between air and ground demonstrated aviation's flexibility. For example, when Montgomery was ready to break through the Mareth Defensive Line, all three air support forces concentrated for the task. The No. 242 Group left the British First Army, joining up with the XII Air Support Command of the II Corps to conduct a campaign against the German aircraft and airfields that might challenge the

British ground advance. The two forces kept enemy air occupied so that the Western Desert Air Force could concentrate all its resources on assisting the advancing army. Fighter-bombers even carried out the commonly eschewed low-level attack operations on German ground troops. Shortly afterwards, the Desert Air Force was reassigned from Montgomery's forces to help the American and British forces in northen Tunisia. Writing to the tactical air forces, Alexander said that "without your support this drive would just not have been possible."[49]

Following the principles of flexibility, concentration, and primacy of theater interests, at times the close air support resources were transferred to coastal patrol missions. The Allies fully expected that they would shortly push the Axis out of Africa. Partly, this was predicated on an expectation of stopping the German resupply from Sicily, Sardinia, and Italy. Using radar and communications intercepts, the air forces tried to choke off support to surviving German forces in North Africa, which maintained a tenacious defense to the end. Airmen hoped that the interdiction might force a surrender. In fact, Germany lost hundreds of aircraft and tons of shipping in three months of heavy action, but supply did not cease entirely. Interdiction was obviously less than completely successful when the Axis chose to put an almost endless effort into a final defensive stance, but interdiction greatly weakened the Axis and forced their early surrender.[50]

Eisenhower remarked that the new Mediterranean tactical organization "solved one of the most basic problems of modern warfare--how to apply air power most effectively to the support of land operations." He also saw that the corps and division commanders in combat would not be as pleased with the new order: "Direct support of ground troops is naturally the method preferred by the immediate military commander concerned," but his vision did not extend beyond the local battle. It did not consider "the competing demands of individual commanders on a far-flung battlefront, each of whom would naturally like to have at his disposal some segment of the Air Force for his own exclusive use."[51]

Concerns continued, personality and misunderstanding very much in tow. Stukas continually attacked Allied ground forces, although by April Axis aircraft were either destroyed or pulled out of the Tunisian campaign. The most celebrated case involved Patton and Coningham. On 1 April, while Patton was serving as commander of II Corps, his troops were bombed by enemy aircraft in a morning-long attack. He complained that the lack of air cover allowed the Germans to bomb all his division command posts and many supporting units.[52]

Coningham, angered by the tone of Patton's report, replied with his own report criticizing the bravery of the II Corps when the enemy attack resulted in only six American casualties. He suggested that the II Corps might not be battle worthy. The sharp personal exchange captured the attention of their senior commanders, including Eisenhower and his chief air deputy, Tedder. Eventually both Coningham and Patton were reprimanded for their bad manners and ordered to meet face to face. The high-level air-ground team remained tense for a time.

Investigation of the incident illustrated the parochial interests in battle. Patton criticized the air support commanders for lack of fighter cover and particularly for their failure to stop an enemy tank advance. Williams, commander of the XII Air Support Command, claimed bad weather prevented the takeoff of aircraft designated for the job. He had even called the Western Desert Air Force for help, but he had cancelled the proposed mission when he heard that Patton's artillery had the tanks under control. Later in the Tunisian campaign, Patton admitted that he was generally getting good close air support. Spaatz reported that the lack of radar coverage and the separation of Patton's headquarters from Williams' contributed to the problem. He took Williams and Patton's chief of staff out to the Eighth Army and Western Desert Air Force to show them how a successful joint operation worked.[53]

Poor communications continued to be a serious factor throughout the Tunisian campaign. Spaatz urged increased employment of air support parties, assigned to ground forces, to call in requests and guide the ground commanders in air support methods. He hoped that some help could be derived from the light bombers that carried radios. Perhaps they could make air-ground contact and hit targets identified by the air support parties. Unfortunately, the more effective close air support fighter-bombers could not carry the heavy radios necessary for good air-ground communications. The latter still consisted primarily of ground smoke or colored panels if definite landmarks were not available.[54]

Spaatz and Coningham gave individual attention to the sensitive air support situation. They tried to instill a practice consistent with concepts evoked at higher levels. Spaatz explained, in a letter to Arnold, how much personal effort by the air commanders was required to keep the peace between the strong-willed air and ground commanders. On one occasion Spaatz noticed that the centralized communications system operated from Alexander's 18th Army Group headquarters did not work adequately. Coordination was required both ways, up the command as well as down. Ground and air commanders needed to actively share problems and activities. In mid-April, after replacing Patton as commander of II Corps, Bradley expressed concern about the lack of aerial photographs and reconnaissance. Spaatz agreed that ground forces had not been given much observation support; most reconnaissance missions had sought intelligence for air force needs. Spaatz thought that he had found the problem in an ineffective air liaison officer assigned to II Corps. He asked Kuter to assign a more senior officer for the rest of the Tunisian campaign.[55]

By May Allied air forces, including the determined close air support units, helped the Allied ground forces corner 270,000 Axis troops in northeast Tunisia. Allied air finally dominated the Axis air forces, compelling all but a few scattered fighter units to operate from Sicily and Italy. In some ways the Allied offensive, including the air-ground cooperation, was remarkable, especially given one of the original concerns when undertaking TORCH--that American troops were not ready for major operations. Estimates of required air support in October 1942 had depressed everyone in the Washington and London planning circuits. The War Department had half expected North Africa to be a relatively safe place for advanced training, but the maneuvering of a combined Allied force proved to be difficult for inexperienced ground and air personnel.

Some field generals were dubious about the adequacy of their air support. Neither the XII Air Support Command nor the combined Allied air forces could guarantee them protection from disruptive enemy air attack. Enemy aircraft over the battlefield diminished in number but continued their attacks, nonetheless, until the end of operations in May 1943. Division commanders often would get air support under the centralized command arrangement. Corps and army commanders could not depend on timeliness of requested air support. Friendly air support often proved ineffective in dislodging the defense-minded Axis ground forces, and air observation of enemy movements was not effective until the air forces could allocate enough escort fighters for the reconnaissance flights.

Air leaders were pleased with changes in air support organization and operational tactics. Greater understanding of aircraft limitations and capabilities by ground leaders, centralization of air support resources, and prioritization of missions allowed the air commander to exercise the accepted principles of air warfare better. The XII Air Support Command commander, Williams, reported that his forces were integrated into the larger theater air concerns, as well as those of the ground commanders he served. In his report on operations Williams noted that he and his principal staff officers "lived and operated with the Corps Commanders during most of the period." While a strong consensus pervaded the joint command posts, sometimes staff officers had to argue out issues. Williams stated that his air staff gave consideration to ground commanders who had urgent requests for close air support. The air support parties provided the communications system and had the experts to give ground commanders advice on the spot. Basically the airmen ran the air support operation, 80 percent of the support missions originating from their operations center. Both Fredendall and Patton had advised Williams not to wait for close air support requests: "You know what the situation is, just keep pounding them."[56]

Introduction of the fighter-bomber, fighters with bomb racks and extra armor, promised more effective attacks on the small well-protected targets favored by the ground forces. The new aircraft type, developed from combat experience, was also important as a symbol for the joint air-ground operations team. The close air support portion of the theater tactical air forces now had an aircraft specifically identified for ground attack. The air support command no longer relied only on fighter and light and medium bomber units that were also responsible for other Army Air Forces missions. Furthermore, now close air support was a more clearly defined mission of the theater tactical air forces, even if it held a lower priority than air superiority and battlefield isolation missions.

The military and civilian leaders in Washington and London and the commanders in the Mediterranean Theater were generally pleased with close air support doctrine and practice, even though the debate over allocation of resources and precise points of force control continued among staff officers. Eisenhower appreciated the new centralized, more personal style of air support, although he worried that he was not effectively transmitting his thinking to the field commanders. New doctrinal points did not flow systematically through successive commanders. American inexperience, individualized field generalship, differing opinions about command, and enduring prejudices prevented a smooth transfer of close air support lessons. Much might be blamed on poor coordination of doctrine between theater and field staffs. The different viewpoints of theater and field and those of brigade, division, and corps levels were not bridged successfully. Inadequate command and control systems caused problems. The newly declared independence of the air forces, at a time when tactics and organization for air warfare were changing rapidly, put additional strain on the air-ground relationship. Air and ground leaders had to continue the struggle of forming a cooperative combat team.[57]

Endnotes—Chapter II

1. John Terraine, A Time For Courage: The Royal Air Force in the European War, 1939-1945 (New York: Macmillan, 1985), pp. 337-51; Wesley Frank Craven and James Lea Cates, eds., The Army Air Forces in World War II, 7 vols. (Chicago: University Press, 1948-58), vol. 2, Europe: TORCH to POINTBLANK, August 1942 to December 1943 (1949), pp. 9-40; Craven and Cate, Plans and Early Operations, 1:339-41; Rpt, Maj Gen Lewis H. Brereton, 3 Nov 42, sub: Direct Air Support in the Libyan Desert, USAFHRC Microfilm Collection, 145.96-64, MAFB.

2. Craven and Cate, Europe: TORCH to POINTBLANK, 2:22-27.

3. Operation Memo no. 17, 13 Oct 42, sub: Combat Aviation in Direct Support of Ground Units, Allied Force Headquarters (AFHQ), USAFHRC Microfilm Collection, 103.2808, MAFB.

4. Ibid.

5. Ibid.

6. Ibid.

7. Dwight David Eisenhower, The Papers of Dwight David Eisenhower, ed. Alfred D. Chandler, Jr., 5 vols. (Baltimore: John Hopkins Press, 1970), 2:874; George F. Howe, Northwest Africa: Seizing the Initiative in the West, United States Army in World War II (Washington, D.C.: Office of the Chief of Military History, Department of the Army, 1957), pp. 32-88; Craven and Cate, Europe: TORCH to POINTBLANK, 2:41-66; I. S. O. Playfair et al., The Mediterranean and the Middle East, History of the Second World War: United Kingdom Military Series, 6 vols. (London: Her Majesty's Stationery Office, 1954-73), vol. 4, The Destruction of the Axis Forces in Africa (1966), pp. 110-28.

8. Craven and Cate, Europe: TORCH to POINTBLANK, 2:50-66.

9. Eisenhower, Papers of Dwight David Eisenhower, 1:445 and 474 and 2:837; Msg, Adjutant General, WD, to CGs, 1 Oct 42, sub: Reassignment of Army Air Force Units, USAFHRC Microfilm Collection, 651.271, MAFB; Ltr, Maj Gen George S. Patton, Jr., to Brig Gen J. K. Cannon, 10 Oct 42, sub: Letter of Instructions, USAFHRC Microfilm Collection, 650.01-2, MAFB; Craven and Cate, Europe: TORCH to POINTBLANK, 2:50-66.

10. Memo, Arnold to Asst CofS, OPD, WD, 16 Jul 42, sub: Tactical Command of Army Air Units, H. H. Arnold Manuscript Collection, box 114, LOC.

11. Eisenhower, Papers of Dwight David Eisenhower, 1:445 and 474 and 2:837; Msg, Adjutant General, WD, to CGs, 1 Oct 42, sub: Reassignment of Army Air Force Units, USAFHRC Microfilm Collection, 651.271, MAFB; Ltr, Maj

Gen George S. Patton, Jr., to Brig Gen J. K. Cannon, 10 Oct 42, sub: Letter of Instructions, USAFHRC Microfilm Collection, 650.01-2, MAFB; Craven and Cate, Europe: TORCH to POINTBLANK, 2:50-66.

12. Ltr, Brig Gen James H. Doolittle to Maj Gen George S. Patton, sub: Torch Air Support, 13 Sep 42, USAFHRC Microfilm Collection, 650.430-1 MAFB.

13. HQ Center Task Force Plans, annex 5, "Paratroop Plan and Air Support Plan," 4 Oct 42, USAFHRC Microfilm Collection, 650.03-2, MAFB.

14. Craven and Cate, Europe: TORCH to POINTBLANK, 2:67-85; Howe, Northwest Africa, pp. 97-253.

15. Ibid.; Commander-in-Chief's Dispatch, North African Campaign, 1942-1943, AFHQ, USAFHRC Microfilm Collection, 621.101-4, MAFB.

16. Howe, Northwest Africa, pp. 277-346; Craven and Cate, Europe: TORCH to POINTBLANK, 2:78-85.

17. Howe, Northwest Africa, pp. 277-98; Playfair, Destruction of the Axis Forces, 4:165-91; F. H. Hinsley, British Intelligence in the Second World War, 2 vols. (London: Her Majesty's Sationery Office, 1984), 2:475-93; Craven and Cate, Europe: TORCH to POINTBLANK, 2:107-08.

18. Craven and Cate, Europe: TORCH to POINTBLANK, 2:78-91; Greenfield, Army Ground Forces and Air-Ground Battle Team, p. 19; Howe, Northwest Africa, pp. 373-76; Rpt, Maj Gen Terry Allen, HQ, 1st Inf Div, 25 Dec 42, sub: Lessons From Operation Torch, USAFHRC Microfilm Collection, 621.549-3, MAFB; Ltr, Brig Gen Paul M. Robinett to Marshall, North Africa, 8 Dec 42, H. H. Arnold Manscript Collection, box 42, LOC.

19. Howe, Northwest Africa, pp. 277-98; Playfair, Destruction of the Axis Forces, 4:165-91; Hinsley, British Intelligence in the Second World War, 2:475-93; Craven and Cate, Europe: TORCH to POINTBLANK, 2:107-08.

20. Craven and Cate, Europe: TORCH to POINTBLANK, 2:78-91; Greenfield, Army Ground Forces and Air-Ground Battle Team, p. 19; Howe, Northwest Africa, pp. 373-76.

21. Howe, Northwest Africa, pp. 383-84; Craven and Cate, Europe: TORCH to POINTBLANK, 2:106-12; Arthur William Tedder, With Prejudice: The War Memoirs of Marshall of the Royal Air Force, Lord Tedder (Boston: Little, Brown, 1966), p. 370.

22. Howe, Northwest Africa, pp. 376-82; Craven and Cate, Europe: TORCH to POINTBLANK, 2:108-12.

23. Rpt, HQ, Twelfth Air Force, Brig Gen Hoyt S. Vandenberg, CofS, 6 Jan 43, sub: XII Air Support Command, USAFHRC Microfilm Collection, 168.7043-5, MAFB.

24. Rpt, HQ, XII Air Support Command, Brig Gen H. A. Craig, Cdr, 6 Jan 43, sub: General Plan of Air Support in Operation "SATIN," HQ XII Air Support Command, USAFHRC Microfilm Collection 168.7043-5, MAFB.

25. Craven and Cate, Europe: TORCH to POINTBLANK, 2:132-45; Howe, Northwest Africa, pp. 374-87.

26. Interv, Intelligence Service, USAAF, with Maj Gen L. E. Oliver, 5 Feb 43, USAFHRC Microfilm Collection 650.03.3, MAFB.

27. Craven and Cate, Europe: TORCH to POINTBLANK, 2:132-45; Memo, Maj Gen Carl Spaatz, 17 Jan 43, Carl Spaatz Manuscript Collection, box 10, LOC; Martin Blumenson, Kasserine Pass (Boston: Jove, 1966), pp. 84-86.

28. Howe, Northwest Africa, pp. 383-84. Craven and Cate, Europe: TORCH to POINTBLANK, 2:142-45.

29. Howe, Northwest Africa, pp. 386-400; Craven and Cate, Europe: TORCH to POINTBLANK, 2:142-43; War Department Basic Field Manual 31-35, Aviation in Support of Ground Forces, 9 Apr 42.

30. Quoted words from Eisenhower, Papers of Dwight David Eisenhower, 2:904-05 and 981-82. See also Howe, Northwest Africa, pp. 396-400.

31. Eisenhower, Papers of Dwight David Eisenhower, 2:904-05.

32. Craven and Cate, Europe: TORCH to POINTBLANK, 2:142-45; Howe, Northwest Africa, pp. 397-98; Report on Operations Conducted by XII Air Support Command, USAAF, Tunisia, 13 Jan 43 to 9 Apr 1943, p. 22, USAFHRC Microfilm Collection, 350.01-2, MAFB.

33. Unless otherwise noted, discussion of the Kasserine Pass operations is based on Craven and Cate, Europe: TORCH to POINTBLANK, 2:113-15, 153-66, 418; Howe, Northwest Africa, pp 401-59 and 492-95.

34. 18th Army Group Operation Instruction no. 3, 1 Mar 43, USAFHRC Microfilm Collection, 612.4300, MAFB.

35. Directives, Northwest Africa Tactical Air Force, 2 Mar 43, subs: The Employment of Air Forces in Support of Land Operations and Formation of Tactical Bomber Forces, USAFHRC Microfilm Collection, 612.4501, MAFB; Excerpts from HQ, MTAF, Report on Operations During the Campaign in Tunisia, USAFHRC Microfilm Collection, 614.4300, MAFB.

36. Some Notes of the Use of Air Power in Support of Land Operations, Intro by B. L. Montgomery, December 1944, USAFHRC Microfilm Collection, 168.6006-137, MAFB.

37. Report of Tunisian Operations, XII Air Support Command, 10 Apr to 13 May 43, USAFHRC Microfilm Collection, 651.3069-1, MAFB.

38. Tedder, <u>With Prejudice</u>, pp. 397-401.

39. Report of Tunisian Operations, XII Air Support Command, 10 Apr to 13 May 43, USAFHRC Microfilm Collection, 651.3069-1, MAFB.

40. Rpt, Spaatz, March 1943, sub: Ground Air Support, USAFHRC Microfilm Collection, 612.4501, MAFB.

41. Futrell, <u>Ideas</u>, p. 69;

42. War Department Field Manual 100-20, Command and Employment of Air Power, 21 Jul 43.

43. Ibid.

44. Ibid.

45. Ibid.

46. Eisenhower, <u>Papers of Dwight David Eisenhower</u>, 2:1107 and 1196; Infantry School "Air Ground Training," <u>The Mailing List</u>, July 1943, pp. 1-38.

47. Craven and Cate, <u>Europe: TORCH to POINTBLANK</u>, 2:170-71.

48. Press Conference, Brig Gen Laurence S. Kuter, 22 May 43, USAFHRC Microfilm Collection, 614.505, MAFB.

49. Ibid.

50. Craven and Cate, <u>Europe: TORCH to POINTBLANK</u>, 2:145-53, 174-75, 182-96.

51. Dispatch, Commander-in-Chief's Dispatch, North African Campaign, 1942-1943, AFHQ, USAFHRC Microfilm Collection, 621.101-4, MAFB; Albert F. Simpson, "Tactical Air Doctrine: Tunisia and Korea," <u>Air University Quarterly Review</u> 4 (Summer 1951): 7.

52. Tedder, <u>With Prejudice</u>, pp. 409-12; Craven and Cate, <u>Europe: TORCH to POINTBLANK</u>, 2:176-77.

53. Craven and Cate, <u>Europe: TORCH to POINTBLANK</u>, 2:145-53, 174-75, 182-96; George S. Patton, Jr., <u>The Patton Papers</u>, ed. Martin Blumenson, 2 vols. (Boston: Houghton Mifflin, 1972-74), vol. 2, <u>1940-1945</u> (1974), pp. 203-08; Maj Gen Carl Spaatz Diary, April 1943, Spaatz Manuscript Collection, box 11, LOC.

54. Report of Tunisian Operations, XII Air Support Command, 10 Apr to 13 May 43, USAFHRC Microfilm Collection, 350.01-2, MAFB.

55. Spaatz Diary, April 1943, Spaatz Manuscript Collection, box 11, LOC; Greenfield, Army Ground Forces and Air-Ground Battle Team, pp. 45 and 51.

56. Report of Operations Conducted by XII Air Support Command, USAAF, Tunisia, 13 Jan 43 to 9 Apr 43, USAFHRC Microfilm Collection, 350.01-2, MAFB.

57. Martin Blumenson, Mark Clark (New York: Congdon & Weed, 1984), pp. 64-70 and 118; War Department Field Manual 100-20, Command and Employment of Air Power, 21 Jul 43, p. 9.

EPILOGUE

Eventually, the campaign in North Africa would be viewed as a sideshow to important campaigns that followed in Europe. For Americans, as well as the British, it was a serious training ground, offering both practical experience and valuable training in modern warfare. Even before the final Axis surrender in Tunisia the air leaders, Tedder, Spaatz, and Coningham, were writing their views of close air support for the Sicily campaign plans. Eisenhower and other Allied leaders broadly supported the third-priority concept for close air support and the need to gain air superiority before another invasion. Both before and during the early stages of the ground campaigns in Sicily and Italy Coningham's tactical air forces joined missions with Doolittle's strategic air forces to work on the first priorities, gaining air superiority and hampering the Axis supply lines.

It remained to be seen how leaders viewed air support in this and other campaigns, how theater commanders concurred or differed with the principles and practices developed in North Africa, how the heightened interplay of air and ground doctrine was sorted out. Would the strong expression of air force tactical air principles survive? Would aircraft builders be able to answer the call for an effective fighter-bomber or observation aircraft, or would the vicissitudes of battle conditions change the requirements? Would communications technology provide better air-ground and command systems? Would better joint training, as promised by McNair and Arnold, help the relationship between air and ground personnel? With all the promises of improvement, how would close air support practices differ from those in North Africa?